FIGS

Copyright © C. Thornton 2014

The right of C. Thornton to be identified as author of this work has been asserted in accordance with the Copyright, Designs and Patents Act, 1988.

All rights reserved. No part of this book may be reproduced or transmitted by any person or entity (including Google, Amazon or similar organisations) in any form or by any means, electronic or mechanical, including photocopying, recording or by any information storage and retrieval system, without prior permission in writing from the publisher.

National Library of Australia Cataloguing-in-Publication entry

Author: Thornton, C., author.

Title: Figs / C. Thornton.

ISBN: 9781925110128 (paperback)

Series: Rare and heritage fruit cultivars ; Set 1, no. 13.

Notes: Includes bibliographical references and index.

Subjects: Fig.
Fig--Varieties.
Fig--Heirloom varieties.

Dewey Number: 583.962

ABN 67 099 575 078
PO Box 9113, Brighton, 3186, Victoria, Australia
www.leavesofgoldpress.com

RARE AND HERITAGE FRUIT
CULTIVARS #13

FIGS

C. Thornton

- RARE AND HERITAGE FRUIT -
THE SERIES

SET #1
RARE AND HERITAGE FRUIT
- CULTIVARS -

1 Apples
2 Cider Apples
3 Crabapples
4 European Pears
5 Nashi Pears
6 Perry Pears
7 Apricots
8 Peaches
9 Nectarines
10 European Plums
11 Japanese Plums
12 Cherries
13 Figs
14 Cactus & Dragon Fruits
15 Oranges
16 Lemons
17 Limes
18 Mandarins & Grapefruit
19 Kumquats, Calamondins & Chinottos
20 Rare & Unusual Citrus
21 Nuts
22 Berries & Small Fruits
23 Quinces
24 Guavas & Feijoas
25 Table Grapes
26 Wine Grapes
27 Avocados
28 Rare & Unusual Fruits

and more...

SET #2
RARE AND HERITAGE FRUIT
- GROWING -

1 Propagating Fruit Plants (other than grafting)
2 Grafting and Budding Fruit Trees
3 Planting Fruit Trees and Shrubs
4 Care of Fruit Trees
5 Pruning Fruit Trees and Shrubs
6 Training and Espaliering Fruit Trees and Shrubs
7 Harvesting and Storage of Fruit
8 Pests and Diseases of Fruit Trees and Shrubs

SET #3
RARE AND HERITAGE FRUIT
- PRESERVING -

1 Preserving Fruit (drying, crystallizing, bottling etc.)
2 Making Cider
3 Making Perry ('pear cider')
4 Making Wine from Fruit
5 Making Fruit Spirits and Liqueurs
6 Making Fruit Schnapps

www.leavesofgoldpress.com

With sincere thanks to
'the fig curators of Australia' -
Peter Allen, Neil Barraclough, Jim Dawson,
Bill Hankin, Deborah Porter, John Rance and
Tony and Julie Stevens.

ABOUT RARE AND HERITAGE FRUIT[1]

This book is one of a series written for 'backyard farmers' of the 21st century. The series focuses on rare and heritage fruit in Australia, although it includes much information of interest to fruit enthusiasts in every country.

For the purpose of this series, rare fruits are species neither indigenous to nor commercially cultivated in any given region.

'Heritage' or 'heirloom' fruits such as old-fashioned varieties[2] of apple, quince, fig, plum, peach and pear are increasingly popular due to their diverse flavours, excellent nutritional qualities and other desirable characteristics.

It is much easier for modern supermarkets to offer only a limited range of fruit cultivars (i.e. varieties) to consumers, instead of dozens of different kinds of apples, pears etc. During the 19th and early 20th centuries, however, the diversity was huge. Old nursery catalogues were filled with numerous

---

1   *Note: this introduction is identical in every handbook in the Rare and Heritage Fruit series.*

2   *The correct term in this case is 'cultivars'; however most people are more familiar with the term 'varieties' and although it is not strictly accurate, we use the terms interchangeably in this series.*

named varieties of fruits, nuts and berries, few of which are available these days.

What are heritage fruits? 'An heirloom plant, heirloom variety, heritage fruit (Australia), or (especially in the UK) heirloom vegetable is an old cultivar that is "still maintained by gardeners and farmers particularly in isolated or ethnic communities".[3]

'These may have been commonly grown during earlier periods in human history, but are not used in modern large-scale agriculture. Many heirloom vegetables have kept their traits through open pollination, while fruit varieties such as apples have been propagated over the centuries through grafts and cuttings.'[4]

Broadly speaking, heritage fruits are historic cultivars; those which have initially been selected or bred by human beings and given officially recognised names, before being propagated by successive generations of growers, retaining their genetic integrity far beyond the normal life-span of an individual plant; those which are not protected by a private plant-breeders' licence, but instead belong to the public at large. They are the legacy of our ancestors; living heirlooms; part of humanity's horticultural, vintage and culinary heritage.

Fruit enthusiasts around the globe are currently reviving our horticultural legacy by renovating old orchards and identifying rare, historic fruit varieties. The goal is to make a much wider range of fruit trees available again to the home gardener.

This series of handbooks aims to help.

---

3   Whealy, K.: 'Seed Savers Exchange: preserving our genetic heritage'. Transactions of the Illinois State Horticultural Society 123: 80–84. (1990).
4   'Heirloom plant' Wikipedia. Accessed 2013.

STORIES

Like people, every fruit cultivar has a name and a story. Take the Granny Smith apple, for example - the most successful Australian apple, instantly identifiable with its smooth green skin, exported world-wide, and now cultivated in numerous countries.

This famous cultivar began in the 1860s as a tiny seedling that chanced to spring up in a compost heap. An orchardist by the name of Mrs Maria Ann Smith lived with her ailing husband in Eastwood, New South Wales (now a suburb of Sydney). She was in her late sixties, a hard worker and the mother of many children.

One autumn day, as usual, Maria Smith drove her horse-drawn wagon home from the Sydney markets, where she had been selling the fruit from her orchard. The wagon possibly contained a few wooden crates she had purchased after selling her produce, in which to transport the next load of wares. One or two leftover Tasmanian-grown French Crab apples might still have been lying in the crates, somewhat battered and past their prime. Imagine 'Granny' Smith, her grey hair tucked up inside her bonnet, trudging down to the creek from which the household drew its water and dumping their decaying remains on its banks.

There in that damp spot, sinking into compost-rich soil, the apple pips lay throughout the winter months. Come spring, one of them split open and a tiny white rootlet appeared. It swiftly bored downwards, stood up and threw off its black seed-case, revealing two perfect, green cotyledons.

The leaves quickly multiplied as the seedling grew, Maria spied it next time she walked down to the creek, the hems of her long black skirts rustling through the ferns. She nurtured the infant tree until it grew up and bore fruit. When at last she picked the first green-skinned apple and took a bite, she must have been surprised by the crisp, hard flesh and sharp taste. No doubt she used it to make pies and other desserts for her sick husband and numerous grand-children, thus discovering that this new cultivar was good for both cooking and eating.

She shared the apples with friends and neighbours, allowing them to cut scion-wood from her tree and graft their own cloned versions. Locally, word of the apple's qualities spread.

'Smith died only a couple years after her discovery, but dozens of Granny Smith apple trees lived on in her neighbours' orchards. Her new cultivar did not receive widespread attention until, in 1890, it was exhibited as 'Smith's Seedling' at the Castle Hill Agricultural and Horticultural Show. The following year it won the prize for cooking apples under the name 'Granny Smith's Seedling'.

'The apple became a hit. In 1895 the New South Wales Department of Agriculture officially recognized the cultivar and began growing it at the Government Experimental Station in Bathurst, New South Wales, recommending its properties as a late-picking cooking apple for potential export.

'During the first half of the 20th century the government actively promoted the apple, leading to its widespread acceptance. However, its worldwide fame grew from the fact that it was such a good 'keeper'. Because of its excellent shelf life the Granny Smith could be transported over long distances in cold storage and in most seasons. Granny Smiths were exported in enormous quantities after the First World War, and by 1975 forty percent of Australia's apple crop was Granny Smiths. By this time the apple was being grown extensively elsewhere in the southern hemisphere, as well as in France, Great Britain and the United States.'

'The advent of the Granny Smith Apple is now celebrated annually in Eastwood with the Granny Smith Festival.[5]

---

5   'Granny Smith' Wikipedia. Accessed 2013

Fruit cultivar stories continue to arise in the 21st century. From AAP, February 21, 2010, 'Mudgee Farmer Bruce Davis Creates New Fruit':

'Is it a plum? Is it a peach? It's probably a pleach as it's a morph of the two tasty stone fruits. Whatever it is, it's a love child of the two, accidentally created by a retired N.S.W. farmer.

'Bruce Davis from Mudgee in the state's central west couldn't believe it when he discovered he had grown a cross between a peach and a plum. The fruit looks like a peach from the outside, but resembles a red plum when bitten into. 'The unusual fruit is believed to be the first of its kind ever grown in the state.

'Mr Davis grows peach and blood plum trees alongside each other and believes the peach/plum tree may have grown from compost that contained plum seeds.

'"It's a really interesting piece of fruit and it's very tasty," Mr Davis said.

'A cross between a plum and an apricot, known as a pluot, has been grown in the past, but a peach and a plum is a new combination for N.S.W., Primary Industries Minister Steve Whan said.

'Industry and Investment N.S.W. Mudgee horticulturist Susan Marte said this was the first time she had heard of anyone accidentally crossing the two fruits.'

NAMES

The origins of the Mudgee pleach and the Granny Smith apple are two of many intriguing fruit stories, but sometimes the name - or names - of cultivars tells yet another story, an etymological one. Names may be inspired by the place a new cultivar was discovered, by the person who selected or bred it, by the shape, flavour, colour or use of the fruit, by an event that took place around the time of discovery, by somebody's sweetheart, or any number of other factors.

Names, too, may be multiplied.

The Granny Smith apple was discovered after the advent of newspapers. If you forgot what the prize-winning cultivar was called, you could look it up and there it would be, in black and white. This was not the case for many ancient cultivars.

The Granny Smith apple's probable mother, the French Crab, itself boasts twenty-six listed synonyms, probably invented by forgetful apple-growers.

Another instance of numerous synonyms is the French cider apple whose name is Calville Rouge D'Hiver, meaning 'Calville Winter Red'. It arose in the late 1500s, and as its popularity spread across Europe, the first thing that happened was that people translated the name into their own language: 'Teli Piros Kalvil', 'Roter Winter Calville, 'Calvilla Rossa di Pasqua', 'Cerveny Zimni Hranac' etc.

Next, when absent-minded peasants could not remember the name of this excellent red fruit, they gave it another one. Imagine a weather-beaten farmer in some isolated French village scratching his beard and musing, 'It was something to do with "Calville". 'Calville Rouge,' perchance?' Across the valley in another village, a cider-brewer was knitting his (or her) puzzled brow and saying, 'It was something to do with winter, I am thinking, or was it autumn? "Pomme d'Automne"?' Further afield, a third Frenchman shrugged his shoulders and declared, 'Devil take me if I can remember how it is called, but it is big and red like the heart of a bull, so let us name it '"Coeur de Boeuf".'"

Fanciful, perhaps, but this might explain why, on the database of the UK's National Fruit Collection, there are more than a hundred synonyms listed for Calville Rouge D'Hiver.

Words are forever evolving. Even when cultivar names stay the same, the language around them is changing and their original meaning becomes lost in the mists of time.

One example of this is the grape cultivar Cabernet Sauvignon, which is considered a relatively new variety, being the product of a chance 17th century crossing between Cabernet franc and Sauvignon blanc.

'Cabernet franc' can be etymologically traced back to 'French Black Grape' (from the Latin word 'caput' which means 'black vine'). The word 'Sauvignon' is believed to be derived from the French 'sauvage', meaning 'wild' and to refer to the grape being a wild grapevine native to France. 'Blanc,' of course, means 'white'. 'Cabernet Sauvignon' no longer means 'Wild Black Grape' in modern French - that would translate as something like 'Vigne Noir Sauvage'. The ancient cultivar name has now taken on its own meaning and is virtually synonymous with the wine made from it.

It is interesting to compare typical cider apple names with, say, typical peach or perry pear names. French words abound among heritage cider apple cultivars, reflecting their roots in medieval Normandy. To the ears of English-speakers these names may sound rather mysterious and aristocratic, until you translate them: for example, Gros Bois, Jaune de Vitré, Moulin à Vent du Calvados, Noël des Champs, Belle Fille de la Manche, Petite Sorte du Parc Dufour and Groin D'âne translate respectively as Big Wood, Yellow Glass, Windmill of Calvados, Christmas Field, Beautiful Girl of the English Channel, Small Kind of Park of the Oven and Donkey's Groin.

Some names of heritage perry pears give us an insight into the bawdy, rustic humour of the perry-drinking English peasants who originally selected them; Ram's Cods, Startle Cock and Bloody Bastard to mention a few.

Heritage grape cultivars have names that come from all over Europe, particularly France and Italy.

Figs go back even further. Humans were cultivating them around 9400 BC, a thousand years before wheat and rye were domesticated. Their names, in English at least, are often drawn from their colour and their place of origin - Brown Turkey, White Adriatic, Black Genoa, Pink Jerusalem, Green Ischia ...

Peaches, a more 'modern' fruit in terms of their popularity and breeding, often bear invented names with fancy spellings, such as Florda Glo, Earligrande, Harbrite and Dixigem.

'IMMORTAL' DNA

Another major difference between stone fruit and fruits such as grapes, figs and apples is their ability to grow 'true' to their parents from seed. Stone fruits are far more homozygous than their ancient cousins the pomes (apples, pears etc.) and the grapes. Growers do graft them, but if you plant their seeds the new tree will bear fruit that's fairly similar to that of the parent tree. This means that the centuries-old grafting traditions, the fierce cherishing, the careful bequeathing and the meticulous labelling that accompany pome fruits, grapes and other heterozygotes are not seen as often in the world of peaches and nectarines. This is why many of their cultivar names seem so different, arising as they do from highly organised commercial breeding programmes of the 20th and 21st centuries.

Unlike the seedlings of say, peaches and nectarines, seedling apples are an example of 'extreme heterozygotes', in that rather than inheriting DNA from their parents to create a new apple with those characteristics, they are instead significantly different from their parents.'[6] (Humans are rather like apples in that way, though not as extreme.)

Returning to our green-skinned Australian apple - 'Because the Granny Smith is a chance (and rare) mutation, its seeds tend to produce trees whose fruit have a much less appealing taste. To preserve the exact genetic code of any plant variety, a stick of the wood has to be 'cloned'. It has to be grafted

---

6   Lloyd, John and Mitchinson, John *QI: The Complete First Series – QI Factoids (2006)*.

onto new roots (or planted directly into the ground, but this is uncommon for trees). Thus, all the Granny Smith apple trees grown today are cuttings of cuttings of cuttings from the original Smith tree in Sydney.'[7]

Cloning by grafting means that the heritage trees - and shrubs - which have survived through the years are genetically identical to their ancestors. Indeed, the heritage plants of today possess exactly the same genetic code as the original trees that arose centuries ago in Asia and Europe. For example, another heritage apple cultivar, 'Court Pendu Plat', is thought to be 1500 years old - the oldest one in existence. Introduced into Europe during Roman times, the living wood from that same tree flourishes to this day, right here in the Great Southern Land.

RARE AND HERITAGE FRUIT IN AUSTRALIA

Many of the rare and heritage fruits that exist in Australia today are clonally descended from plants brought to our shores by the early European settlers, when few, if any, quarantine laws existed. Good luck rather than good stock monitoring limited the number of plant diseases unintentionally imported during the early days of colonization. Fortunately, by 1879 it was recognised that in order to prevent the introduction of serious pests and diseases, quarantine measures were needed. In 1908, the Commonwealth Quarantine service came into operation and took over local quarantine stations in every Australian state.

However, before 1879, there was no limit to the varieties of fruiting plants that could be imported into this country. Many of those old genetic lines survive to this day but sadly, many others have been lost.

---

7   *Stirzaker, Richard: Out of the Scientist's Garden: A Story of Water and Food. Collingwood, VIC: CSIRO Pub. (2010).*

Fortunately, Australia is one of only two countries free of fire blight, a serious and ineradicable disease that wiped out millions of apple, pear, loquat and quince trees in Europe and the U.S.A. during the 1900s. This means that when certain heritage cultivars went extinct elsewhere, they remained safe in this country. Some have now been restored to their region of origin, now grafted onto fire blight-resistant rootstock.

Over the course of the decades since 1879 Australian fruit growers imported (through quarantine) the latest new cultivars bred by overseas agricultural research stations. Year by year, as scientific advances in breeding and genetics were made, the older cultivars fell out of fashion and were swept aside in favour of the new. They, too, became part of our almost forgotten fruit inheritance.

COMMERCIAL CULTIVARS

Naturally, plant breeders strive to provide the products demanded by the market. Commercial orchardists want to purchase heavy-bearing trees with high disease resistance, whose fruit ripens all at the same time to save on picking costs. Wholesalers want fruit that keeps in storage for a long time without spoiling, and can be shipped without damage. Only firm-fleshed, bruise-resistant fruit will survive modern-day processing. After harvesting, apples, for instance, are tipped into crates, then passed along a conveyor belt through machinery that washes and brushes them clean of insecticides and dirt. This process removes some of the fruit's natural protective coating, so the machines re-apply a commercial grade wax before polishing them to a high shine and pasting a plastic label onto each one. Then the apples are packed into cartons for shipping to markets and stores.

Supermarket shoppers demand visually attractive fruit - large, regular in shape, unblemished and with highly coloured skin. Consumers also choose fruit with extra sugar content and juiciness.

All these characteristics, nonetheless, do not necessarily give rise to the best flavour or nutrition. To pick a tree-ripened fruit from your own back yard and bite into it is to experience the taste of fresh food as our forefathers knew it. Growing and preserving their own food, unconcerned with transportability and long storage times, they aimed for a wide variety of fruits, each of which had a unique and delicious taste.

Rare fruit, heritage and heirloom fruit enthusiasts across the world are reviving our horticultural legacy by renovating old orchards and sourcing 'lost' historic and unusual fruit varieties. Their goal is to encourage community participation and to make a wide range of fruit trees available again to the home gardener.

This series of handbooks aims to help.

WHY PRESERVE RARE AND HERITAGE FRUITS?

• They provide access to a wider range of unique and delicious flavours.
• We can enjoy the nutritional benefits of fresh, tree-ripened food.
• Biodiversity: The preservation of a wide range of vital genetic material helps to insure against the ravages of pests and diseases in the future.
• They allow a longer harvesting season, with early and late ripening.
• Culture: heritage varieties, with their interesting assortment of names, are living history.

Collections of heritage fruit trees are precious. Anyone who is the custodian of an old tree should treasure it.

Note: It is permitted to bring fig cuttings into Australia, but they must be brought through quarantine to prevent the introduction of serious diseases or insect pests, which could devastate crops nationwide.

www.daff.gov.au/biosecurity

CONTENTS

About Rare & Heritage Fruit ix
About Figs 1
Terminology 21
Key 22
Fig Cultivars A - C 25
Fig Cultivars D - H 51
Fig Cultivars I - N 69
Fig Cultivars O - S 91
Fig Cultivars T - Z 109
Appendix 121
Bibilography..127
Figs in Australia 131
Index 137
Figs by Mail Order 146
Heritage Fruit Groups in Australia 147

HORTICULTURAL SOCIETY'S SHOW.
THE FIRST DAY.

Encouraged by the success of its venture last spring, the Horticultural Society of Victoria has again presented its patrons with an exhibition in the Melbourne Town-hall.

The chief exhibitors on, this stage are Messrs. Taylor and Sangster, Mr. Jas. Scott, Mr. J. C. Cole, Mr. G. Brunning, and Messrs. Thos. Lang and Co.

The fruit classes are somewhat shorn of their usual proportions through the ravages of oidium. Grapes are hardly present at all, but the display of orchard fruits is unprecedented, and the competition unusually severe.

Mr. J. C. Cole enjoys the honour of exhibiting the best general collection ever shown in this colony; his 150 dishes occupy two-thirds of the table on which his relative, and for the nonce antagonist, Mr. H. U. Cole, shows a well-arranged collection of 56 dishes.

From the Horticultural Society's gardens [Burnley], also, came fine collections of fruit, including 142 dishes of apples (deprived of their true character by polishing) 54 of pears, and a few dishes of plums.

Amongst the growers of pears and apples there is a spirited contest. In the open pear class, Mr. T. C. Cole's collection of 38 varieties was placed first, doubtless on account of the large size of the specimens; Mr. Draper's, of 61 dishes, came next, whilst Mr. Harbison's 70 dishes were left unnoticed, although in point of rarity they were remarkable.

For the various fortunes of the combatants in apples, we must refer our leaders to the prize-list. Amongst exhibits worth special mention are a collection of figs, 14 varieties; ...locust heans, which will some day be an article of commerce: and a number of curiously-shaped gourds and cucumbers.

The Argus (Melbourne, Victoria: 1848 - 1957) Thursday 20 March 1873

ABOUT FIGS

The common fig (Ficus carica) is the source of the fruit also called the fig, an important food crop. Probably native to western Asia, it has been sought out and cultivated by man since ancient times, and is now widely grown throughout the temperate world, both for its fruit and as an ornamental plant.[1]

The fig fruit is unique. In fact, it is not really a fruit but a flower turned inside out. This structure is known botanically as a syconium.

Ficus carica was one of the first plants to be cultivated by humans. Nine subfossil figs dating to about 9400–9200 BC were found in the early Neolithic village Gilgal[1] in Palestine. The find predates the domestication of wheat, barley, and legumes, and may thus be the first known instance of agriculture. It is proposed that they may have been planted and cultivated intentionally, one thousand years before the next crops were domesticated. Figs were also a common food source for the Romans.

The importance of figs as a food crop cannot be underestimated in the centuries before canning, bottling and electric refrigeration were invented. Because of their naturally high sugar content, figs could be sun-dried and packed away for later use. The sugar helped to preserve them through the lean

---

1 *'The Fig: its History, Culture, and Curing', Gustavus A. Eisen, Washington, U.S.A. Government Printing Offices., **1901**.*

months - long past the time when households ran out of fresh fruit.

The taste of a good fig, a tree-ripened, freshly-picked fig, is sublime. Many people these days have only ever tried figs bought from a supermarket, and finding the flavour and texture unpleasant, have believed thereafter that they don't like figs. Do not judge figs on the generally poor quality ones available commercially. A ripe, fresh fig should be tender and slightly soft. When you bite into it, a surge of silky, juicy, sweet, rich flavour fills your mouth. It is like jam eaten straight out of the jar, only infinitely more subtle and complex, with overtones of honey and flowers. When you look at the interior of the fruit from which you have taken a bite, you'll see dense fringes of flowerlets lapped in a luscious, glistening syrup.

It is easy to propagate figs. If you plant a fig branch in the ground, especially during the winter dormancy period, a new tree identical to the parent will grow and produce fruit within two or three years. Dormant fig cuttings can stay alive and viable for several weeks if they are kept cool; thus they are easy to transport. Thousands of years ago, human traders introduced figs to regions around the Mediterranean — wherever ships and camels could travel. Over time, new varieties arose and were cultivated in Spain, Portugal, Morocco, Turkey, Greece, Tunisia, France and numerous other countries.

Figs were first brought to the shores of America in the sixteenth century. By the 1700s missionaries from Spain were cultivating them on their farms up and down the west coast of Mexico and California. It was here that a commercial fig industry sprang up in the late 1800s. This evolved into one of the largest centralized fig industries in the world, along with those of Turkey, Italy, Spain and Greece.

Of the thousands of named cultivars, a relatively small number have been selected as the cornerstones of regional fig industries across the globe. The most popular include White Adriatic, Kadota, Mission (Black Mission) and Calimyrna. These are the cultivars most often commercially available during the fig harvesting season, which extends June through December in the Northern Hemisphere and December through June in the southern hemisphere.'

Other popular and widely available cultivars include Brown Turkey, Preston Prolific, Black Genoa and White Genoa.

Fig Types

There are essentially four types, or classes, of edible figs.

CAPRIFIG

The caprifig produces a small, unpalatable fruit; however, the flowers inside the caprifig fruit produce pollen. This pollen is essential for fertilizing fruit of the Smyrna and San Pedro types. The pollen is transported from the caprifig to the pollen-sterile fig types by a blastophaga wasp. Commercial growers hang baskets of blastophaga-infested caprifigs in their orchards so that the wasps can fertilize the fruit.

SMYRNA

The Smyrma (caducous) fig varieties produce large edible fruit with true seeds. For normal fruit development the blastophaga wasp must bring pollen from caprifigs. If this fertilization process does not occur, fruit will not develop properly and will fall from the tree.

Smyrna-type figs are used for dried fig production. The process of caprification is important, as the seeds contribute to the nutty flavour of the dried product.

Cultivars of this class set virtually no breba crop. The second crop develops on the current season's growth and reaches full maturity only when the flowers are pollinated by the fig wasp and the ovules develop into fertile seeds. Figs of this type are distinguished by the large eye in the base of the immature fruit.

SAN PEDRO

Figs of this type generally produce two crops of fruit in one season — one crop on last season's growth and a second crop on current growth. The first crop, called the breba crop, is parthenocarpic and does not require pollination. Fruit of the second, or main crop requires pollination from the caprifig.

The breba crop appears early in the spring on last season's wood. However, the second crop of the Smyrna type may fail to set because of lack of pollination from blastophaga wasps and caprifigs.

Also known as intermediate figs, San Pedro figs are used for noncommercial fresh fig production.

COMMON FIG.

This type of fig develops parthenocarpically, which means 'without needing to be pollinated'. The fruit is mostly produced on the current season's wood, and it does not contain true seeds. The common fig is also known as the persistent fig, and it is used for commercial fresh fig production.

Each year, the common fig normally produces two crops. In spring the first (breba) crop appears on wood from the previous year. It ripens in early to mid summer. The second harvest, which is called the main crop, forms on new season's wood between November and December (May and June in the southern hemisphere). These figs generally ripen between February and June (August and December in the southern hemisphere).

Fig Characteristics

There are hundreds of named cultivars (varieties) of figs. How does one go about telling the difference, and choosing which ones to grow?

SKIN COLOUR

Figs range in colour from virtually black through purple, violet, red, brown, yellow, green and almost white. Some are multi-coloured, patterned with vertical bands or stripes, or spotted. The green varieties are normally reserved for drying.

It is important to know what colour the mature fig is, so that you can tell when it is ripe. Ripe figs become soft on maturity, but if they become mushy or disintegrate, this signifies that they are overripe.

PULP COLOUR

The pulp colour of fig cultivars can range from clear or opaline through cream, honey-colour, amber, gold, strawberry-pink, red, plum and purple.

SIZE AND SHAPE

Figs come in all shapes and sizes as well as colours and flavours. They can be as large as tennis balls or as small as marbles. There are round ones and flat ones. Some are pear shaped and others are like elongated tear-drops. Some have long necks while others have no neck at all.

FLAVOUR

Taste can vary vastly from cultivar to cultivar. Figs can have flavours reminiscent of honey, caramel, strawberry jam, maple syrup or raspberry tart. Taste can range in character from piquant fruitiness to the nutty sweetness of confectionery.

LEAF SHAPE

Leaf shapes may differ in the number of lobes, the amount of scalloping, size, the general outline, stem length and so on.

Fig Crops

It is possible for 'common' and 'San Pedro' figs to produce two crops each year. The first crop is called the breba[2] crop, and it develops in the spring on the previous year's growth.

The main fig crop, sometimes called the second crop or the higos crop ('higos' means 'fig' in Spanish), develops on the current year's growth and ripens in the late summer or autumn. The main crop is usually superior in both quantity and quality to the breba crop; however, some cultivars, sich as 'Mission', are renowned for producing good breba crops.

Growers of cultivars with poor breba crops often discard the brebas before they ripen, to encourage growth of the main crop. In some cold climates the breba crop is frequently destroyed by spring frosts. However, in regions where the summer is too cool for the main crop to set, the breba crop is the only crop that will ripen.[3]

Propagation

Figs can be propagated by cuttings, air layering or grafting. Figs grown from seeds are not true to type.

Most fig trees are propagated from hardwood cuttings. Cuttings can be taken in late autumn or early winter. They should be 20 to 25 cm long and contain several nodes. The base should be cut just below a node.

Site and Soil Requirements

If you want plenty of fruit from your fig trees, give them as much sunlight as possible. Plant them in an area that is sunny for most or all of the day; otherwise, do not expect a bountiful

---

2   *'Breba' can also be spelled 'breva', which has identical pronunciation in Spanish. 'Breva' is an altered form of the Old Spanish "bebra', which comes from the Latin '(ficus) bifera": 'twice-bearing fig'.*

3   *Source: Wikipedia, 'Common Fig'. Retrieved March 2014.*

harvest. Early morning sun is particularly beneficial to fig trees, because it evaporates dew from their leaves, reducing the risk of mould and other diseases. Good drainage is even more essential than richly composted soil. Plant your fig trees on a site where water stands for no more than twenty-four hours after it rains. If figs are planted in waterlogged ground, their roots will not receive enough oxygen and many will perish. The tree will be stunted and will eventually die.

Pests and Diseases

Fig trees are extremely hardy, however like all plants they have their predators.

Queensland fruit fly (Dacus tryoni) is a troublesome pest in the northern states of Australia, including many areas of N.S.W. Use pheromone traps to attract and kill male flies, and clean up any fallen fruit.

Fig blister mite (Aceria ficus) can attack the interior of the fruit, creating brown, dry patches. Destroy any fruit that has been damaged this way, to prevent other fruits being infected as they mature.

Fig rust and anthracnose are fungal diseases that mainly affect trees growing in coastal areas, Fig rust shows up as powdery yellow spots on the leaves. Anthracnose shows up as small brownish black spots that gradually expand. Leaves affected by either of these diseases will turn yellow before dropping from the tree. Control fungus with copper-based fungicides.

Fig mosaic virus creates a mottled pattern on the leaf. Infected plants should be destroyed.

Other pests that can affect figs (as well as other plants) include root knot nematode (Meloidogyne spp.) and dried fruit beetle (Carpophilus spp.)

Figs in Australia

In 2001 Bill Hankin, pomologist and organic farmer, prepared an inventory of figs in Australia for the Heritage Seed Curators. He has kindly given permission to quote from his work, 'Figs in Australia'.

'There are 112 varieties listed in the following Inventory. The first figs came to Australia in 1788 with the First Fleet. Cuttings of 'Large Blue' and 'Long White' were brought to N.S.W. on the first fleet. Officers sent to the new colony also bought fig cuttings when the fleet stopped at the Canary Islands on the way to Australia. Keith Smith notes that there were 'Canary Island' type figs growing in Governor King's orchards at Parramatta, west of Sydney, in the 1840s.

'During the later part of the 19th century, especially after the gold rushes, there was great uncertainty about which cultivars of fruit would succeed in the Australian colonies. In response fruit nurserymen made concerted effort to import as many different varieties of fruits from the rest of the world as quickly as possible. Cuttings of a large numbers of fig cultivars were imported from all over the world.

'In 1873 the fruit nurseryman John J. Cole of Richmond near Melbourne in Victoria, offered 26 varieties of figs that had already been grown and fruited, plus another nine varieties that were 'new' and so unproven in the new colony.

'John Goodman at Bairnsdale in East Gippsland offered a wide range of 29 varieties for sale with no descriptions at all in his 1910 wholesale catalogue.

'Among these varieties were Smyrna type figs which need insect pollination to set fruit. This lead to the fig wasp being brought to Australia. It was introduced at the instigation of Baron Von Mueller, the director of the Melbourne Botanic Gardens in the 1870s and 1880s.

'During the 1870s till the 1890s the Victorian Horticultural Society (later the Royal Victorian Horticultural Society,

R.V.H.S.) arranged for the importation of a large number of fruit varieties. Approximately 75 fig varieties were among these shipments. This program was funded by R.H.S.V. membership. Many of these members were nurserymen but others were enthusiastic amateur 'gentlemen' who wished to have prior access to rare varietal material. The trees were firstly established at the Society's trial gardens at Burnley, close to Melbourne. Later when the trees were established scion material was distributed to members.

'George Neilson's three reports of 1873, 1874 and 1875 list all the fruits imported and lists the cultivars that had been established. These gardens were the source for many of the fig trees later introduced into nursery catalogues around Australia.

'Unfortunately we have no records of who received such scion material, where it was planted and if it survived. Many of these figs varieties are now presumed 'lost'. But it is possible that some of them were alternative names (synonyms) for varieties still in existence in Australia or overseas.'

Meanwhile, it had not taken the early European settlers long to discover that the conditions in Western Australia were extremely favourable for growing fruit.

The City of Gosnells is an area in the southeastern suburbs of the Western Australian capital city of Perth. Around the year 1880 Stephen Gibbs, the son of English immigrants, was living there with his wife, on a property called Hillside Farm. Stephen began to take up extensive properties, mainly for dairying. He established an orchard in the 1890s. When he died in 1928 at the age of 80, his son William and lived at Hillside.

Bill Hankin continues: 'The First World War had a huge impact on the nursery trade. There was a severe shortage of workers especially in rural areas, as about half a million men joined the Australian armed forces. Probably demand for fruit trees dropped also as the war disrupted farm exports. By 1916 there were only six fig varieties offered in Goodman's catalogue. This diversity was never recovered.

'In the period after the War the focus for all orcharding changed to growing fruit varieties which would keep and could be exported to Great Britain. Figs being primarily a soft fresh fruit became mainly a garden fruit in Australia. In 1934 Goodman offered just five varieties of fig. In 1989 four varieties were being sold.

'But other fig varieties were being grown. Since the 1890s Italian, Greek, Spanish Serbian, Macedonian and other immigrants from Mediterranean countries have brought fig varieties to Australia. This process increased during the 1950s and 1960s. But these cultivars were largely smuggled in and did not go through the normal quarantine processes. And there is a strong reluctance by migrants who have done this to discuss what varieties they are growing. Frequently these varieties came from home villages and have no published established variety names.

'During the early 20th. century, state governments established research fruit orchards. One of the functions of these orchards was to be repositories of a wide range of fruit cultivars. The monograph by R. Ikin of the CSIRO published in 1974 reflects this effort to preserve a range of horticultural diversity.[4]

Nonetheless, towards the end of the 20th century the number of known, named fig cultivars in Australia dwindled rapidly. At this point it is useful to interrupt Bill's account with some insights by kind permission of John Rance of Rare Fruit South Australia:

---

4 R. Ikin Ph.D. *Varieties of Fruit trees, Berry Fruit, Nuts and Vines in Australia. Australian Government Publishing Service Canberra, 1974.*

'It just doesn't figure that the dependable fig tree, the fruit tree most valued by our pioneering forefathers, has become to this generation, the forgotten fig. Once esteemed and cherished, it has now become a fruit of inconvenience. A whole generation of kids is growing up without ever tasting a fresh fig, or even knowing what they look like.

'[19th century] fig connoisseurs would gather together, to discuss and vote on the delicate differences between their many varieties. In some parts of Europe the science of growing the fig to perfection had become an art worth bragging about.

'So what happened between then and now to lower the fig's status, from up there rivalling the apple, to so low that our kids have never seen one. Has the fig changed so much? Or have we changed so much? Why is it so rare to find fresh figs at the fruit and veg. stall or in the supermarket? And if you do find them, they are nothing to rave about anyway. Are they so hard to grow? No, I can't think of any fruit tree that is less demanding or so easy to grow. So what has happened?

'The answer in a nutshell is, we have become creatures of convenience rather than pursuers of quality. The emphasis has shifted from 'what is best for the consumer' to 'what is the best for the supplier'. This ideal back yard tree is not an ideal commercial orchard tree. The fig may hold its place in history, but it can't hold its place on the shelf. The fig may ripen to perfection on the tree, but it won't hold perfection on the shelf. There are lots of things the [commercial] growers don't like about figs, and some things the supermarkets don't like about them, but as a back yard tree they out-perform all else.'[5]

(Bill Hankin points out that since he wrote that piece, things have somewhat changed for the better and the fig is gradually making a commercial comeback.)

---

5   *Rance, John. The Fignificent Forgotten Fig.*

At Gosnells in Western Australia, the Gibbs family eventually sold Hillside farm, and 'in the early 1990s the state education department was granted a 40% share of the property, with the rest to be used by other groups. The idea was to provide a community farm that promoted ecological and sustainable living practices through education and recreation opportunities.'[6]

We now skip to the twenty-first century. The city of Perth has expanded vastly in the last 70-odd years, and Hillside Farm's orchard is being utilised as a gene pool for a fruit cultivars, according to a paper presented by Mr Alex Hart at A.C.O.T.A.N.C.[7] 2001. Mr Hart was a member of The Western Australian Nut and Tree Crop Association (W.A.N.A.T.C.A.[8]). Presumably, W.A.N.A.T.C.A. was one of the community groups using Hillside's resources.

In his paper 'Problems Identifying Fig Varieties', Mr Hart wrote about 'the varieties planted in the gene pool at Gosnells Hillside Farm'. He lists many different fig cultivars which the amateur fruit enthusiasts of W.A.N.A.T.C.A. had managed to preserve. Somehow, many of these cultivars have since made their way into the hands of private fig collectors across the country, growers who have faithfully labelled them and propagated them, sharing them with others, so that these unique varieties might live on, virtually immortal, a gift for generations as yet unborn.

In South Australia, the Rare Fruit Group was involved in a similar rescue mission, as described in Bill's article:

'The South Australian fig repository at Loxton reportedly had some 17 varieties in it in 1994. I say reportedly because the state government then decided as a cost cutting measure

---

6   *Government of Western Australia Heritage Council.*
7   *The Australasian Conferences On Tree And Nut Crops*
8   *A wonderful organisation, regrettably now defunct.*

to close down this and other heritage orchards. The figs were bulldozed and the land sold off.

'Fortunately, before the destruction was complete, members of the South Australian Rare Fruit Association were invited to take cuttings to propagate on the fig varieties at this orchard. Other varieties from a government orchard in Alice Springs in the Northern Territory have also become part of this collection. Currently members of the S. A. Rare Fruit group have some 45 fig varieties growing in the gardens and orchards. But many of these are undocumented and undescribed.'

Again from *The Fignificent Forgotten Fig,* by John Rance: 'Across Australia the fig tree collections are being destroyed. The Agricultural Research Stations are no longer studying the potential of the fig. The humble fig has been sentenced to commercial doom. This is despite the fact that it is better suited to South Australian and Western Australian growing conditions than almost any other fruit tree.

'Before the Loxton collection was destroyed, [members of S.A. Rare Fruit] were able to acquire cuttings of each of their 18 varieties. These have been distributed amongst interested members, several members taking full collections.

'Since this initial collection we have collected further material from around Australia. We have new varieties from Perth in Western Australia, Gosford in New South Wales, Darwin and Alice Springs in the Northern Territory, and Mt. Gambier in South Australia.

'Our collection now stands at around 40 varieties, making it by far Australia's largest gene-pool. It is important that we keep track of as many of these cultivars as possible, for many were on the verge of being lost completely-and many others would have become untraceable. As we can sort out and grow-on these new varieties we hope to make them available to the members.'

To continue with Bill Hankin's 2001 introduction: 'A list of some varieties was published in the Rare Fruit Group

Newsletter three years ago. The Association hopes in time to build up a database of information about the varieties being held by members.

'John Rance of the S.A. Rare Fruit Association has especially helped greatly with this Fig Inventory by sharing information about varieties being grown by the group. So has Graham Brookman of the Permaculture inspired farm called 'The Food Forest' at Gawler in South Australia. Graham offers a number of fig varieties for sale that are unavailable elsewhere in Australia.

'In the early 1990s the East Gippsland Organic Association started a project to preserve heritage fruit varieties. This started a major effort to preserve heritage apple varieties but was expanded later to take in fruits like pears, plums and figs. This effort included a series of grafting days every winter in Victoria. After 1997 this effort was sponsored by the 'Heritage Fruits Group'[9] of Permaculture Melbourne and led to many rare fruit varieties including rare figs being preserved and propagated within the Permaculture movement across Australia. In fact it is among permaculturally inclined growers and gardeners that the desire to preserve heritage varieties is strongest.

'As part of this work a list of heritage fig varieties was compiled by Permaculture Melbourne's 'Heritage Fruits Group' [now the Heritage Fruits Society]. This list was then placed on the Permaculture Melbourne web site. All the references in this inventory to varieties being grown by the Royal Horticultural Society of Victoria in 1896 at Burnley come from the fig list on the Permaculture Melbourne web site.

'In 1900s the Museum of Victoria in Melbourne commissioned the creation of sets of wax replicas of fruit varieties grown in Victoria at the time. These wax replicas sets still exist and are in the custody of the Science Works Museum in

---

9   *Now the Heritage Fruits Society.*

the West Melbourne suburbs of Spotswood. Among them is a collection of four painted wax replica figs which reputedly are very accurate. The fig list compiled by the Permaculture Melbourne web site also incorporates this information. The references to wax models in this inventory of fig varieties are based on this work, as I have not been able to see them myself.

'One cause for optimism is that fig trees once established can be extremely long lived. For example the oldest known fig tree in the world was planted in Cuzco in 1540 by Pizzarro when the Inca empire was destroyed by the Spanish Conquistadors. A fig tree planted in the grounds of Lambeth Palace by Cardinal Poole in 1525 at the time of Henry VIII lived into the 1900s. In South Australia figs planted in the 1880s at Martindale Hall near Mintaro have survived without care since the 1950s. It is extremely probable that there are other examples of these heritage fig varieties to be found in abandoned orchards and in old gardens around the Australian countryside. It is a matter of looking, if possible identifying them, and taking scion cuttings!

'Just recently I visited a Permaculture garden in a southern suburb of Adelaide. There in the backyard was a huge, magnificent fig tree planted according to the owner, many decades ago. The fruit reportedly is dark skinned and quite small, but it was also very distinctive in its growth habit: low and spreading with very short internodes between the branches. Perhaps in time it will be identified! That is one of the practical benefits that hope will flow from this exercise.'

Bill Hankin, HSCA, 17/6/2001

TONY STEVENS' FIG COLLECTION

As the 20th century drew to a close, John Rance of Rare Fruit S.A. was compiling a collection of fig cultivars, both 'heritage' and new. One of the rescuers who had collected fig scion from the doomed orchards of Loxton, he was bent on expanding his range.

Finding genuine 'heritage' figs is a difficult task, partly because nurserymen sometimes fail to correctly label cultivars. Furthermore it is not easy to identify figs purely by their characteristics. Apart from the fact that they can look very similar in leaf and fruit, the growth of a single cultivar can actually vary from place to place and year to year, depending on the season and the local geography/climate.

The only sure way to identify heritage figs would be to employ DNA analysis, which is prohibitively expensive.

As the publicity officer for Rare Fruit S.A., John often spoke on local radio. Whenever he did so, he would broadcast requests for people who were growing outstanding but unknown fig varieties to contact him. When anyone did so he would visit their garden to see the tree for himself, enquire about its history and (in harvest season) sample the fruit.

If his enquiries left him satisfied that the cultivar was a seedling, and not grown from a cutting of an existing tree, he knew he had stumbled across a new cultivar worthy of being named and cloned. He then obtained cuttings. Usually he named the fig after the owners of the tree.

Over the years, his fig collection grew; in fact it overflowed his suburban garden, which became cluttered with innumerable potted trees. That was when his friend and fellow member of Rare Fruit S.A., Tony Stevens, offered to take it over.

John readily moved his entire collection to ten acres at Gawler, South Australia, the home of Tony and his wife Julie. Not only did permaculture enthusiast Tony tend the trees (now planted in the ground), he also carried on the fig-hunt with enormous enthusiasm.

'Look for old settlements, old orchards and ruins,' John advised. 'Collect cuttings of any ancient fig trees that have survived. These gnarled old veterans, planted by discerning pioneers, are likely to bear excellent fruit.'

Tony visited country towns from South Australia to New South Wales and south-west Queensland, searching for lost and 'new' figs. Sometimes he would work on local farms, in exchange for bed and board.

By 2009 Tony was growing a large number of varieties from all over Australia which had either lost their names or never had a name, in addition to many 'rescued' named cultivars. He nurtured around seventy individual trees with more than 100 grafts, which - it was thought - would encompass between thirty and forty varieties when they were all finally identified.

Tony meticulously labelled and cross-referenced everything he collected, at pains to identify everything correctly.

'I'm pretty sure I have several instances of the same fig with two or three names,' Tony told John, 'but I can't be sure until they've fruited for a few seasons ...'

'Without DNA testing the task is truly formidable,' John replied. He suggested giving the unknown ones temporary names, just to distinguish them, until their real identity was discovered.'

And that's what happened.

In association with the South Australian Rare Fruit Society Tony undertook a project which sought to establish a register of varieties true to name and with good descriptions as they grow in Australia. After waiting until the trees matured enough to bear fruit and comparing the fruit with images and descriptions, he managed to identify many of the cultivars in his collection.

Some trees stubbornly refused to fruit, or were too young to fruit because they had been grown from small cuttings. In the meantime, Tony provisionally named them after the location at which he had collected them, or for some other association. Other cultivars in his collection had fruited but did not match the descriptions or images of any known varieties. These, which might be seedling trees (and thus new cultivars), Tony also named provisionally, bearing in mind that it might take a few more years to establish their true identity.

Tragically, Tony passed away in 2009 and his precious fig collection fell to the care of his widow, Julie. Tending such a vast number of trees is a mammoth task, in which she is aided by volunteers from Rare Fruit S.A.

In 2011 permaculture practitioner Deborah Porter journeyed from Melbourne to Gawler after gaining permission to obtain scion wood from the Stevens collection. She took cuttings from every tree. Returning to Melbourne with 110 named and un-named cultivars, she shared duplicates of every one with Peter Allen of Telopea Mountain Permaculture Farm. Deborah's goal is to establish her own heritage fig collection at Beechworth in Victoria.[10]

OTHER AUSTRALIAN FIG COLLECTIONS

Meanwhile, in Victoria's Gippsland region, Neil Barraclough had rescued several more named varieties as part of the East Gippsland Organic Association's heritage fruit preservation project, and in Western Australia, another fig enthusiast had privately collected a total of almost forty.

This Western Australian collection comprises some figs that have found their way from Tony Stevens' collection; some cultivars donated by Mrs Margaret Beck, whose surname was possibly bestowed on one of them; by W.A.N.A.T.C.A.[11]

---

10   *With thanks to Deborah Porter for providing details.*
11   *Western Australian Nut And Tree Crop Association (a*

founder and president David Noel; from Mr Collins, whose name is attached to two more cultivars; and by Alex Hart, who obtained them from the Stoneville Research Station.

STONEVILLE RESEARCH STATION

In the early 1970s apple breeder John Cripps (born 1927) convinced Western Australia's Department of Agriculture to begin a limited program whose aim was 'to breed new apple varieties suitable to Western Australian environmental conditions'. This commenced in 1972 when the state government opened the Stoneville Research Station. Researchers evaluated more than 1600 seedlings and eventually narrowed them down to one standout apple, which they called 'Cripps' Pink'. This was later renamed to 'Pink Lady' - an apple that became a multi-million dollar Australian success story.

The research station expanded to become the state's main fruit research facility. A wide range of fruit tree varieties was grown there, including numerous named, heritage figs.

From 1989 the apple breeding program was gradually relocated to the Manjimup Horticultural Research Institute, and in 2004 Stoneville was closed down entirely. As happened at South Australia's Loxton, the heritage fruit trees were bulldozed. After they were torn from the ground the land was subdivided into residential allotments.

Prior to the destruction of the trees, a few private growers obtained propagation material. Many of these were WANATCA members, and Alex Hart was one of them. They planted clones of these figs in a community orchard at Hillside Farm.

The fig cultivars noted in this book are drawn from all these lists put together; the government research station databases, the Stevens collection, the other private collections and the old nurserymen's catalogues. Many of these rare and heritage figs are now lost (perhaps growing in your backyard?) but thanks to foresight and determination on the part of a few rescuers, many are still alive, healthy and identified.

---

wonderful organisation, now unfortunately defunct).

To help you on your fig quest, we have listed retail sources for many of the cultivars. Many scarce, recently-rescued figs are currently in private collections and not available to the public; however, as the trees mature there is a good chance that cuttings will be offered for sale by rare and heritage fruit groups at some time in the future.

Terminology

* Crenate; scalloped or notched.
* Decurrent; running or extending downward along the stem.
* Eye; the eye of a fig is an opening at the apex of the fruit (the ostiole) where the skin draws together. Closed eyes prevent bacteria, fungi and insects from entering the fig and causing problems.
* Globose; ball-shaped, spherical.
* Lineate; marked with lines, especially parallel lengthwise lines; striped.
* Oblate; (of a spheroid) flattened at the poles.
* Obovate; egg-shaped and flat, with the narrow end attached to the stalk.
* Opaline; exhibiting a milky iridescence like that of an opal.
* Pyriform; pear-shaped.
* Subcordate; approaching a heart shape.
* Truncate; shortened.
* Turbinate; (especially of a shell) shaped like a spinning top or inverted cone.

Key

 A 'lost' fig cultivar. Possibly still growing in Australia, but unidentified.

 A fig cultivar that has been positively identified and is known to be growing in Australia, but is in the care of private growers.

 A fig cultivar that has been positively identified and is commercially available.

Rare and Heritage Fig Cultivars

in Australia
A to C

A Bois Jasper

Once grown at the Royal Horticultural Gardens, Richmond Park, Burnley, Victoria, in 1896. No description. Whereabouts now unknown.

Adam

Synonyms: Adam's, Black Adam, Dauphine.

Provenance: Acquired from South Africa, but apparently a French variety.[1] Introduced into Australia by the Royal Horticultural Society of Victoria (RHSV) in the 1890's at Burnley. Listed in the Law Sumner & Co catalogue of 1915. Sold commercially by Brunnings as an 'early good dark fig with a large breba crop'. Sold by Goodman's until the early 1950's. Ikin states that it was in the Victorian, Western Australian and N.S.W. State fruit Collections in 1974.[2] Hart lists it as being grown at Gosnells Hillside Farm, W.A., in 2001.

Skin colour: Green to yellowish--brown skin turning red to violet or purple-black when fully ripe.

Pulp colour: Flesh is juicy, thick and creamy white, changing through champagne and pink to red as it ripens. The pulp is darker red when pollinated.

Description: The fruit is oblate, with a short stalk. Medium to large in size. A good, high quality fruit.

Breba Crop: Reliable, heavy, high yield

Other information: A San Pedro type fig. The tree is large and vigorous. Height is around 4 m while width is also about 4 m. The foliage is dramatic, as the leaves are very large. 'San Pedro figs are not grown commercially in N.S.W.

| 1 | *Figs 4 Fun* |
| 2 | *Rare Fruit Society of South Australia* |

The only variety available in N.S.W. is Adam (also called Dauphine).[3] San Pedro varieties set a breba crop without pollination. However, to produce a main crop pollination with a Capri fig is required. 'Adam' usually produces a useful Breba crop around Christmas time in South Australia and a major crop in February. Prefers temperate climate.

Tree Sources (as of publication date): All Green, Food Forest, Yalca.

Ficus carica 'Adam'. Image: Figs 4 Fun

 ADRIATIC, BLACK

This cultivar was found in Western Australia, however its source prior to this discovery is unclear. It exists in private collections and growers have not yet been able to provide images or descriptions.

---

3   *'Fig growing in N.S.W.', by N.S.W. Agriculture:*

 ADRIATIC, WHITE

Synonyms: Adriatic, Verdone, Verdonne, Fragola, Strawberry Fig, Grosse Verte, Chico, Strawberry, Italian Strawberry, Nebian, Ventura, Fico De Fragola, Strawberry Jam Fig, Dalmation Fig.

Provenance: Central Italy. Listed at Burnley, Victoria, in 1896, and old fruit catalogues. Still common in cultivation.

Skin colour: Greenish, chartreuse, tinged with yellow or amber when ripe. Later main crop is blushed with purple.

Pulp colour: An attractive light strawberry to deep pink or deep red. If pollinated the flesh turns a bright ruby red.

Description: The main crop fruit is medium to large, spherical to conical, with a delicious flavour. Turbinate with small or no neck. Thin skin. Peels very easily when ripe. When tree-ripened, this fig is unsurpassed, with its rich strawberry flesh.[4] Described by Schum, 1950 as 'filled with strawberry jelly'. Ripens in February (Australia).

Breba Crop: White Adriatic usually produces no breba crop or only a small number of breba fruit

Other information: The tree is of medium vigour with a low, spreading habit. Has the largest leaves of any variety. 'Large, vigorous tree leafs out 7 to 10 days earlier than other varieties, thus more subject to spring frost injury. Has capacity to initiate new growth and produce some crop in frost years. Prune to force new growth. Railton's catalogue of 1880 states that variety ripens in February in Victoria. Has been available commercially in Australia since the 1880's and is still widely available from nurseries. Popular in England, where it is known as Grosse Verte. Used in California's dried fig industry.

Fruit is excellent eaten fresh, makes good jam or paste, and is a good fig for drying. The small breba crop has light chartreuse skin, later main crop is blushed with purple. If pollinated the flesh turns a bright ruby red. White

---

4   Daleys Nursery

Adriatic has been grown in the Murrumbidgee Irrigation Area (MIA) for canning, jam and drying[5]. 'Performs well in warmer areas and is well suited to drying. The fruit matures in February and March.'[6]

'This fig is another one of [chef] David Arnold's recommendations - he says that of all the figs he grows, this one impresses people the most. Sometimes called the strawberry jam fig, in reference to its sweet jelly like red flesh, excellent flavour and flesh quality, a curiosity with this variety is that the early crop on the tree tends to be fruit with light coloured skin, and the later crop is more dark blushed, trees have very large leaves.'[7]

Tree Sources (as of publication date): Yalca, Food Forest, Daleys.

Ficus carica 'White Adriatic'. Image: A$ Dibble Plants, NZ

---

5   *'Fig growing in N.S.W.', by N.S.W. Agriculture.*
6   *Daleys Nursery*
7   *Yalca Fruit Trees*

 AGEN

Agen is a synonym of Verdal, whose other synonyms are Verdala, Grosse Verdale, Verdal Longue, Agen D'Agen, Grosse du Draguignan, and Ficus carica virescens 'Risso'. Verdal is unavailable in Australia.

This cultivar was listed by George Neilson in 1874 as being grown at the RVHS gardens at Burnley. Lost.

Agen was one of the varieties imported to the U.S.A. from England by John Rock in 1883. Brebas are rare with this cultivar.

Main-crop figs are medium sized, up to 1-3/4 inches long and 1-7/8 inches in diameter, turbinate to obovate; with short, thick neck; average weight 43 grams; stalk thick, up to 1/2 inch long; ribs narrow, slightly elevated; eye medium, open, scales chaffy, tinged with violet; surface somewhat glossy, with prominent bloom; white flecks large, conspicuous; skin checking crisscross at maturity; colour green, tinged with violet or light brown; meat thin, white; pulp strawberry; flavour rich; quality good.

Caprified figs are medium to large, oblate - spherical; colour attractive, greenish violet; bloom especially prominent; pulp solid, dark strawberry, rich in flavour. Considerably better in size, appearance, and quality than uncaprified fruit. Season: late.[8]

 ALMA

Synonyms: Fall Gold, White, Italian White.
Provenance: Once source states: 'Bred by Texas A & M University, and released in 1940'. Another source reports: 'A 1974 Texas Agricultural Experiment Station introduction. '

---

8   *Fig Monograph - California Agriculture by by Ira J. Condit., 1933*

Skin colour: Golden-brown.

Pulp colour: Amber

Description: A small to medium fig golden-brown, pyriform (pear-shaped) fig with amber pulp. Sweet and delicate flavour. Fruits are of excellent quality, being succulent and sweet, with barely noticeable seeds and with a well sealed eye.

Breba Crop: no information

Other information: Highly resistant to fruit rots. Wood is very hardy. This very productive, compact tree is cold hardy and has a prolonged spring dormancy.

Sources: Alma is in Tony Stevens' collection and is being grown in Australia by private fig enthusiasts.

 ANGÉLIQUE

Mentioned in the *Australian Town and Country Journal* in 1892; 'Amongst the older and better known varieties of figs in [the collection of The Universal Nursery Company, Wahroonga] is the Angélique...'

Now lost.

ANGÉLIQUE NOIR

'Synonyms: Melette, Petite Figue Grisé, Coucourelle Blanche, Madeleine, Early Lemon, Figue d'Or.

See also 'Bordeaux'.

'There are many descriptions of this variety. Confusion has existed as to its identity, as well as its synonyms.

'The tree is moderately vigorous, bearing two crops. Breba crop fair to small; fruits medium, up to 2 inches in diameter, turbinate spherical; neck very short and indistinct; stalk 1/4 inch long, swollen toward the apex; ribs present, narrow; eye large, open, scales chaffy, bordered with pink, often brightly coloured; surface waxy or glossy; colour lemon yellow, with white flecks few and inconspicuous; pulp light strawberry, hollow at the center.

'Second-crop figs very similar in appearance to the brebas, but smaller in size; average weight 32 grams; shape oblate-spherical, without neck; stalk up to 3/4 inch long, often curved, and prominently swollen at the apex; fruit of beautiful appearance on account of the waxy surface, bright yellow colour, and rosy eye scales; pulp light strawberry to almost amber, hollow, flavour insipid; quality poor. Very susceptible to insect infestation through the open eye, and to subsequent spoilage.[9]

Once grown at the Royal Horticultural Gardens, Richmond Park, Burnley, Victoria, in 1896.

Whereabouts now unknown.

 ## Aubique Blanche

Once grown at the Royal Horticultural Gardens, Richmond Park, Burnley, Victoria, in 1896. Whereabouts now unknown. Aubique Blanche is a synonym for Grosse Jaune ('Big Yellow') and is also known as Aubico Blanco, Tapa Cartin, and Ficus carica monstrosa Risso.

 ## Aubique Noir

Once grown at the Royal Horticultural Gardens, Richmond Park, Burnley, Victoria, in 1896. Whereabouts now unknown; however Aubique Noir is a synonym for Brown Turkey, so it may not be lost after all.

 ## Archipal

Synonyms: Archipel, Arachipel, De L'archipel, Figue Grise, Ronde Noire, Hardy Prolific, L'archipel, Blanche, Italian Honey, Lattarula, Lemon, White Marseilles, Rust, Conadria.

---

9   *Fig Varieties: A Monograph by Ira Condit (Hilgardia, February 1955)*

Conflicts: Sometimes confused with Neveralla, Osborn's Prolific, Osborne, and Osborn. In the U.S.A. this name appears to belong to a very different cultivar. California Rare Fruit Growers describe it as 'medium to large, skin is dark reddish brown, flesh amber, often tinged pink.' The confusion is exacerbated by the wide range of synonyms, meaning anything from 'Round Black' (Rond Noir) to 'White' (Blanche).

Provenance: Probably France. Hart writes that Australian Archipal stock was 'originally derived from importations from U.S.A. via N.S.W.'

Skin colour: Greenish-yellow. From Rare Fruit S.A.: 'Skin is thin with reddish ribbed stripes, bronze with violet tinge or dark reddish brown'

Pulp colour: Honey/opaline. From Rare Fruit S.A.: 'Pulp is amber coloured, very sweet and almost seedless.'

Description: A medium to large fig with a very thin, edible skin. Resistant to spoilage.

Breba Crop: Good breba crop.

Other information: Early to mid season ripening. A good, reliable bearer. Fruit splits badly in heavy summer rains. 'Fruit has better flavour in cool climates.'[10]

Tree Sources (as of publication date): Food Forest

Ficus carica 'Archipal'

---

10   *Figs 4 Fun*

 BALLONA

From a report in the *South Australian Register*, 1890:

'Francis Mellon, fruit and vine grower, said that before we try to dry the figs we must have the right sort. He produced some figs grown and dried at Dunolly, in Victoria, which had been declared by the largest importer of figs in Victoria to be far superior to anything imported. The name of this fig was Ballona (or 'Goddess of War'). In 1827 he brought out twenty-four of these trees for the Government, and he believed they had been placed in some of the Government establishments. The tree from which the dried figs were produced was brought out from Paris in 1878, and is the best fig of the south of France... The Ballona fig was a trifle better here than in France. He had imported tons of 'Ballona' figs, but they did not equal in flavour those of the same kind grown in Victoria, It seemed that the soil affected the quality of the figs. The tree at Dunolly was 16 feet high, and bore for three months altogether about 2 cwt. [hundredweight][11] of green figs, which would be reduced in drying to about one-fourth. The value of these figs would be a little over one shilling per pound. They were simply dried in the sun.'

Ballona is now lost.

 BARDAJIC

Synonyms: Bardajik. A green fig with a bright red pulp, mentioned in Western Mail, Perth, in 1912.

Now lost.

---

11   In the Imperial system, the long hundredweight is defined as 112 pounds (8 stone), which is equal to approximately 50 kg.

 Beck

Synonyms: Becks. This fig is being grown privately in Western Australia. It may be a cultivar that was donated by Mrs Margaret Beck. No other information is available at this time.

 Belle Dame Blanche

Listed in Goodman's Wholesale Fruit Catalogue of 1910. Condit says, 'Cuttings of Belle Dame Blanche have fruited at Riverside, and all were found to be identical with [fig cultivar] Brunswick.'

Brunswick is grown privately in Australia.

 Betada

Listed by George Neilson in 1874 as being grown at the Royal Horticultural Gardens, Richmond Park, Burnley, Victoria, in 1896. Described by Hogg (1884) as a small, spherical, black fig, with rose-coloured pulp of rich flavour.

Whereabouts now unknown.

 Black Prince

Skin colour: dark purplish black.
Pulp colour: deep red.
Description: A large, elongated, obovate fig. Richly flavoured, sweet, juicy and delicious.
More information: This cultivar is being grown privately in Australia.

Black Adam - see Adam
Black Adriatic - see Adriatic, Black
Black Genoa - see Genoa, Black
Black Ischia - see Ischia, Black
Black Mission - see Mission
Black Provence - see Provence, Black
Black Sicilian - see Sicilian, Black
Black Turkey - see Turkey, Black
Black Uley - see Uley, Black

Blanche Royale

Known only from the wax replica at the Science Works Museum in Victoria. Not referred to in any other literature.

Bluet

Listed in Goodman's Wholesale Fruit Catalogue of 1909 to 1914. No description. Lost.

Bondance Precoce

Grown by the RHSV in the 1890s at Burnley. Lost. A synonym of Franche Paillarde, described and illustrated by Eisen (1901) as a pyriform fig, below medium in size, brown in colour, with light-red pulp of fine quality.

Bordeaux

Synonyms: Albicougris; Angélique Black or Angélique Noire; Figue de Bordeaux; Figue Poire; Figue Aubiquoun; Grosse Rouge De Bourdeaux; Negronne; Petite Aubique; Petite Figue Violette; Violette De Bordeaux; Violette; Aubiquon; Aubique Noire; Aubique Violette; Violette Longue; Violette de Bordeaux.

Provenance: France

Skin colour: Black

Pulp colour: Yellowish red

Description: Described by Crichton as a 'desirable French variety with large long pyriform fruit. The skin black and thickly covered with bloom and when dead ripe splits in lines. flesh yellowish red, tender juicy and sweet. Tree is robust and a moderately good bearer.' This variety was offered in Australia by W C Grey in 1907 and described differently, as: 'Large jet black fruit with deep red pulp of excellent quality.'

No known sources and probably lost in Australia. Still available from Davis California, U.S.A.

Bourjassotte, Black

A synonym for Black Barnissotte. Other synonyms include: Black Barnisaotte, Barnissoto, Barnissotte, Black Bourgassotte, Bourgassotte Noire, Brogiotto Nero, Brogiotto Fiorentino, Grossofigo, Bellegrade, De Bellegarde, Precoce Noire, Ficus barnissote.

A most excellent dessert fig, medium, broader than long, Skin black, pulp is dark, blood red. The interior of the stalk and neck bright yellow. A very late fig. First crop somewhat larger, skin rougher and pulp more yellowish. Rare. Leaves 3-lobed, almost entire with undulating margins of medium size densely covering the branches.

Once grown in Australia. Listed in the Goodmans of Bairnsdale catalogue, 1914, but whereabouts now unknown.

A dark purple fig 'Barnisotte' currently grows at University of California Davis, USA.

Bourjassotte Blanche

Grown by the RHSV in the 1890s at Burnley. Whereabouts in Australia now unknown.

 BOURJASSOTTE GRIS

Synonyms: Grizzly Bourjassotte, Napolitaine.

Hogg (1884) describes this as 'Fruit, about medium size, round, and so much flattened as to be somewhat oblate. Skin, of a chocolate colour, covered with a very thin bloom. Neck, very short. Eye, open. Flesh, of a deep dark blood-red colour, with a thick syrupy juice, and very richly flavoured. A delicious fig; ripe in the end of September [northern hemisphere].'

Grown by the RHSV in the 1890's at Burnley. Listed in Australia in Goodman's Fruit Catalogue of 1911. Figs 4 Fun describes it as 'Fruit 5 cm in length with greenish violet skin darker at the apex. The flesh is red. No source in Australia but is available still in the U.S.A.'

BOURJASSOTTE NOIR

See Black Bourjassotte.

BOURJASSOTTE, WHITE

A hand-painted wax replica of this cultivar exists at Melbourne's Science Museum in Spotswood, Victoria. Whereabouts unknown See also

 BROWN

This cultivar is being offered for sale by Daleys Nursery, who describe it thus: 'A dwarf selection of brown fig, slow growing and compact, this small tree only reaches about 1 - 1.5 m in height. Great for small space and pots.'

Tree Sources (as of publication date): Daleys Nursery, Kyogle N.S.W.

Brown Turkey - see Turkey, Brown.

Brown Ischia - see Ischia, Brown.

 ## Brown Bell

Pyriform in shape, with a long neck, some ribbbing, and brown skin. This cultivar is being grown privately in Australia.

 ## Brown Sugar

This cultivar is being grown privately in Australia; however we have been unable to find information on it. It may be the same as 'Celeste'.

 ## Brunswick

Synonyms: Clementine, Madonna, Magnolia, Black Naples, Bayswater; Brown Hamburgh, Drap d'Or, De St. Jean, Hanover, Large White Turkey, Red. See also Belle Dame Blanche, Boughton.

Provenance: From the U.S.A.. Variety grown in N.S.W. in the 1890s

Skin colour: Violet brown

Pulp colour: Reddish brown

Description: According to Goodman's catalogue of 1917 'Produces large long fruit with violet brown skin. Grown in Texas, U.S.A., since the 1840s under the name Magnolia because of its colour. A fine fig, used for drying.

Other information: Hogg (1884) writes: 'Very large and pyriform... Skin, greenish yellow in the shade, tinged with pale brown on the other side. Flesh, opaline, tinged with very pale flesh-colour towards the centre. A very rich and excellent fig... The tree is very hardy, but not so good a bearer as the Brown Turkey.'

Bull's No 1

Named after 19th century British naturalist and fruit expert Henry Graves Bull. Listed by George Neilson in 1875 as being grown at the RVHS gardens at Burnley. No description. Probably a UK variety. Lost.

Bultajik

Synonym: Bardajik, Bardajic.

Reported in the *Western Mail* Perth, W.A. 1912: 'Several other other valuable varieties of Smyrna have been introduced into this State, including the Bardajic, a green fig with a bright red pulp...'

From the Western Mail, Perth, W.A., 1930: '... though there are hundreds of varieties of figs, many varieties that are good for eating do not make a high-quality dried fig... For a description of the drying varieties I will quote from notes which I made in Smyrna in 1833: "A considerable number of varieties of figs is grown in the Meander Valley, but three varieties of 'green' figs are of special interest, because it is from these that the dried figs are prepared. Mr Edward Whittall gave the native names as Barda jik (from its supposed resemblance to a water jar), Lop, and Shecker (meaning sugar), and said that the Bardajik, which is not a very good cropper, is most highly esteemed as the thinnest skinned, sweetest, and best drying fig. ... Bultajik, an oval thin-skinned fig, is the most highly esteemed fig for eating fresh or drying. This is the same as Mr Whittall's Bardajik; for spelling does not count for much in Turkey.'

Calimyrna

Synonyms: Sari Lopi, Sari Lop, Erbeyli, Lob Injir.

Provenance: Calimyrna is a cultivar bred from Smyrna in California's San Joaquin Valley. Several numbered selections of Calimyrna have been bred over the years. 'Calimyrna' was listed in Alex Hart's 2001 paper as growing at Western Australia's Hillside Farm.

Skin colour: Yellow

Pulp colour: Yellow to amber

Description: The fruits are large, with a large open eye. They are oblate to spherical in shape. Sweet, with a very rich, nutty flavour and tender golden skin. They are said to taste of honey, jam and butterscotch, with a nuttiness from the numerous seeds. Can be eaten fresh, out of hand.

Breba Crop: Calimyrna can produce brebas, but they are seedless and of poor quality.

Other information: The N.S.W. Department of Primary Industries states: 'The Smyrna and the Calimyrna varieties were commonly grown for dried fruit production in the Murrumbidgee Irrigation Area of New South Wales, back in the 1920s. Production of dried Smyrna figs is not common now. These figs require pollination with the fig wasp and caprifigs (caprification). The process of caprification is important in dried fig production, as the seeds contribute to the nutty flavour of the dried product.' Figs drop if not pollinated.

Tree Sources (as of publication date): This cultivar is being grown in Australia but is not as yet being offered commercially.

Ficus carica 'Calimyrna'. Image: The Produce Blog by Rick Chong

 Cape White

Synonyms: Blanche

Provenance: Unknown

Skin colour: Green

Pulp colour: Cream

Description: Medium-sized to small fruit. The fruit is squat and pear shaped, with almost no neck, and slightly ribbed, with a small, open eye. The flesh is cream to white, with a solid centre.

Breba Crop: unknown

Other information: Cape White is a vigorous tree with a low, spreading habit. It was introduced to Victoria from South Australia and was mainly grown for jam. It produces a golden-coloured jam that is more attractive than that of White Adriatic. It grows best in warmer areas. Trees are compact and vigorous. The fruit matures early, in January or February, but is prone to splitting. Listed in Ikin12 in the N.S.W., Victorian and Queensland fruit collections in 1974. (Australia)

Tree Sources (as of publication date): This grows in Australia in private collections.

---

12   See bibliography

 Capri

The Capri fig, whose fruit is generally inedible, is the only fig variety to have both male and female flowers, and is essential for the pollination of the Smyrna varieties. The name caprifig is derived from caprificus (or 'goat fig' in Italian), as it was considered worthless. The fruits are usually dry, pithy and resinous. They are not considered palatable.

Unlike common figs the caprifig produces three crops of synconia. These are known by their Italian terms, profichi, mammoni and mamme. (See appendix)

Tree Sources (as of publication date): This grows in Australia in private collections.

Caprification

(See appendix.)

Carmel Special

Synonyms: Caramel Special.

This round, golden-fruited cultivar is being grown privately in Australia. It was originally collected in Western Australia.

Ficus carica 'Carmel Special', unripe. Date: March, 2014

Cassaba

Synonyms: Cassabah.

A red-fleshed Smyrna-type fig. mentioned in the Western Mail (Perth, W.A.) Saturday 29 June, 1912, Page 6: 'Several other valuable varieties of Smyrna have been introduced into this State, including the Bardajic, a green fig; with a bright red pulp, Cassaba, which also has red flesh, and the Purple Bulletin, a purple fig with a reddish pink flesh.'

'The Cassaba fig is small, of a dark green color, and the pulp is of a highly colored red tint, is for table use and does not dry well.' Page 6, Evening News (Sydney, N.S.W. : 1869 - 1931) Thursday 28 January 1892.

Also described as 'a small, roundish, reddish fig with darkened flesh.'

Now lost.

Castle Kennedy

Provenance: Scotland. An anonymous account in 1865 stated that this variety had then existed at Castle Kennedy for nearly a century; but how it came there or what was its origin were matters on which there was no reliable information. It was believed to be quite distinct from any other variety in cultivation in England.

Skin colour: greenish yellow on the neck and towards the stalk, but pale dingy brown mottled with dull ashy grey on the widest part and towards the eye.

Pulp colour: pale opaline, with slight stains of red round some of the seeds nearest the eye.

Description: Fruit, very large, obovate. Skin, thin, very tender, pulp very tender, but not richly flavoured. A large and handsome early ripening fig.

Other information: 'A writer in the Gardener's Chronicle, November 19, 1864, observed that Messrs. Lawson and Son were to distribute the Castle Kennedy fig, which had obtained an award from the Edinburgh Horticultural Society.

'A letter dated 1954, from Sir John Dalrymple, Earl of Stair, states that two trees of the Castle Kennedy fig are still being grown mainly for sentimental reasons at Lochinch Castle, Stranraer, Wigtownshire, Scotland. Judging from the various accounts of this variety, the Castle Kennedy is very similar to Brunswick, but belongs to the San Pedro rather than to the Common group of figs.'13

Grown at Burnley 1896, Listed in Brunnings 1916. Whereabouts in Australia unknown.

 ## Catalogna

Synonyms: none known.
Provenance: Sourced from Picone Exotic Orchards. Possibly named by John Picone.
Skin colour: dark purple
Pulp colour: unknown
Description: According to Daleys Nursery: 'A shiny dark purple skinned fig with very sweet flesh. Selected by a local fruit grower for the superb quality of the fruit.'
Tree Sources (as of publication date): Daleys.

---

13   I Condit, A Monograph

 Celeste

Synonyms: Hardy Celeste, Conant, Blue Celeste, Celestial, Honey, Improved Blue Celeste, Malta, Sugar, Tennessee Mountain, Violette, Celeste Violette, Little Brown, Little Brown Sugar.

Provenance: Hart reports this cultivar as growing at Hillside Farm W.A. in 2001, and as having come from a source in South Australia.

Skin colour: Light bronze to violet.

Pulp colour: Strawberry/rosy amber.

Description: Small to medium in size. Pyriform shape, with tapering neck. Firm flesh, almost seedless. The 'eye' at the bottom of the fruit is small, keeping insects out. The eye remains green until the fig is almost ripe (unlike Brown Turkey). Very cold-hardy. Delicious fig with rich, very sweet flavour, great for drying (can almost dry on the tree). Also excellent fresh or as preserves. Breaks up when stewed. Sought-after by cooks because they are small enough to preserve whole.

Breba Crop: Yes, but very minimal.

Other information: The tree is large, vigorous and very productive, with big, striking leaves. The main crop ripens early on last year's wood. Do not prune mature Celeste trees heavily because this can reduce the crop. Main crop is heavy but of short duration. Long-lived and hardy. Good for pots. This cultivar is sold commercially in the U.S.A.. Widely adapted, and manageable tree. Celeste is probably the most popular common fig variety for growing in Mississippi, U.S.A. Cold-hardy and resistant to souring and splitting.

Tree Sources (as of publication date): None. This cultivar is being grown privately in Australia.

Ficus carica 'Celeste'. Image: Ison's Nursery & Vineyards

 ## Chemeghour

Listed as growing at Burnley, Victoria, in 1896 Whereabouts unknown.

 ## Citrus

From Tony Stevens' fig collection. Provenance and description unknown. In private collections.

Clancy

From Tony Steven's fig collection. Tony named it after the fictional character 'Clancy of the Overflow', in honour of the fig's geographical origin, the place where he had collected the cuttings. Banjo Paterson's poem 'Clancy of the Overflow' opens with:

> *I had written him a letter*
> *which I had, for want of better*
> *Knowledge, sent to where I met him*
> *down the Lachlan, years ago,*
> *He was shearing when I knew him,*
> *so I sent the letter to him,*
> *Just `on spec', addressed as follows,*
> *`Clancy, of The Overflow'.*

The Lachlan River is located in the Southern Tablelands, Central West, and Riverina districts of New South Wales, Australia.

'Clancy' remains in private collections in Australia.

Clémentine

Listed as growing at Burnley in 1896. Whereabouts unknown.

Another synonym for Brunswick - see Brunswick.

Col Di Signora Blanca

Synonyms: Lucrezia. 'Col di Signora Blanca' translates from the Italian as 'The Neck of the White Lady'.

Hogg (1884) writes, 'Fruit, medium-sized, pyriform, with a rather long neck, and marked with very distinct longitudinal ribs. Skin, thick, green, but changing to yellowish white, and covered with fine grey bloom. Stalk, short and stout. Eye, closed. Flesh, of the darkest blood-red; very thick, syrupy, and most delicious. It shrivels and dries well. One of the finest figs in cultivation.'

Grown at Burnley in 1896. Whereabouts unknown.

Col Di Signora Nero

'Col di Signora Nero' translates from the Italian as 'The Neck of the Black Lady'.

Hogg (1884) writes, Fruit, above medium size, long pyriform, with longitudinal ribs running from the stalk towards the apex. Skin, entirely dark chocolate, covered with a thin grey bloom, and when at perfect maturity cracking into irregular markings. Eye, small and open. Flesh, very dark red throughout, like Col di Signora Bianca and Gros de Draguignan; exceedingly rich and sugary, in fact a perfect conserve. Ripens late.

Grown at Burnley in 1896. Whereabouts unknown.

 ## Collins

Three fig cultivars, 'Collins No. 5', 'Collins No. 3' and 'Collins No. 8' were listed by Hart as growing at Hillside Farm in Western Australia in 2001. Collins has a golden-green skin, with some ribbing.

Private collectors in W.A. and Victoria are growing 'Collins' and 'Collins Seedling'.

 ## Collins Seedling

See 'Collins'

 ## Conadria

Synonyms: Adriatic Hybrid, Verdone, Verdone Hybrid, Red Conadria, Contessina.

Provenance: This is an American hybrid from the renowned fig breeder, Ira Condit. The first artificial hybrid fig in the world, it was released from the breeding program in Riverside, California, U.S.A. in 1956. Conadria is one of Dr. Condit's varieties which were selected on the basis of being crack- and split-resistant. Most have a small eye. All have very high sugar content and are very resistant to decay. See the appendix for more about hybrid caprifigs. Figs 4 Fun reports: 'The University of California has maintained a fig cultivar improvement program since 1922. The 'Conadria' and 'DiRedo' cultivars were released to the industry from this program in the mid 1950s (and the 'Tena' cultivar was selected and released in the mid 1970s). The key to the development of hybrid fig seedlings that are persistent or of the 'common' type came in 1942 when Dr. Ira Condit discovered a unique type of caprifig growing at Cordelia, California. This caprifig, thought to be a European cultivar named 'Croisic', was parthenocarpic and edible, and could pass on the persistent characteristic to a portion of a seedling population developed from it.'

Skin colour: Yellow to light green, with a slight purple blush.

Pulp colour: Strawberry.

Description: A medium to large pyriform fruit - the average weight is 48 grams (1.7 oz.) High sugar content. Juicy, with excellent flavour, sweet and mild. Not as sweet as Kadota, but fruit resists spoilage in rainy weather and has a small, tight eye so it rates well for insect resistance. Skin cracks all over but does not split. Flesh is firm.

Breba Crop: Bears a light to good breba crop.

Other information: Fruits of the second (main) crop are numerous, medium sized, and have a relatively small eye. These figs are good eaten fresh and excellent eaten dried. The tree is vigorous, precocious, long-lived and fairly hardy, with good rebound from freezes. More productive than White Adriatic but of lesser quality. Tree tends to excessive growth under irrigation, best in hot climates.

Tree Sources (as of publication date): Grown privately in Western Australia and Victoria; sourced from Stoneville, W.A.

Ficus carica 'Conadria'. Image: Armstrong Garden.

Rare and Heritage Fig Cultivars

in Australia
D to H

DALGETY

This cultivar is being grown privately in Australia. Sourced from Tony Stevens, and probably named after the place he collected it; Dalgety is a small town in New South Wales, located by the Snowy River, between Melbourne and Sydney.

DATTE

Synonyms: Italian synonyms include Fico Madama Rosso at Milan, Fico Genovese at Pavia and Laggo Maggiore, Fico della Madonna at Bergamo, Fico Rossetto at Voghera, Fico Larde at Alessandria, and Fico Averengo and Fico Datto at Torino. 'Datte' is French for 'date'.

Provenance: Italy. First described in 1817.

Description: Condit (1955) describes Datte as having light green skin and pale strawberry pulp. He writes that the main crop of figs is 'fairly sweet and rich, but dry in texture. Much improved by caprification but generally poor, both fresh and dried.' He goes on to say, 'Breba crop small or none; fruit medium sized or above, colour green, tinged with violet from the underlying violet meat; pulp dark strawberry; flavour good.'

On the other hand Hogg (1887) says, 'Skin, of a dingy brown, or rather a dirty, muddy colour all round the apex, and gradually becoming paler towards the stalk, where it is green. Flesh, dark rose-coloured, thick and syrupy, with a rich flavour-. Excellent.'

Other information: Once grown at Burnley, Victoria. Datte is reported to be common in northern Italy, where the brebas are especially esteemed; in southern districts, second-crop figs are better than brebas.

Whereabouts in Australia unknown.

 ## D'AGEN

See 'Agen'. Grown at Burnley, in Victoria, during the 19th century. Whereabouts now unknown.

 ## DEANNA

Synonyms: Deanne, Deana, Deane. Possibly named after 1930s film star Deanna Durbin?

Provenance: Originated at Riverside, California, U.S.A. through the breeding program of Dr Ira Condit, as a replacement for Calimyrna. All Condit's cultivars were selected on the basis of being crack- and split-resistant; most have a small eye. All have very high sugar content and are very resistant to decay. Hart lists a green-skinned fig called 'Deanne' at Hillside Farm, W.A., in 2001, which may be the same cultivar.

Skin colour: Green to golden-yellow.

Pulp colour: Strawberry pink.

Description: Attractive, medium to large, sweet fruit of high quality, very good flavour. Eaten fresh. Fruit resists splitting, but if it does split it does not decay. Very popular in the U.S.A.

Breba Crop: Yes

Other information: Productive tree. Late ripening.

Being grown privately in the southern states of Australia.

Ficus carica 'Deanna'. Image: Trees of Joy.

 De Lipari

Synonym: Verte Petite. See also Grosse Monstrueuse De Lipari.

Provenance: Lipari is an Italian island of the coast of Sicily.

Skin colour: Green, becoming yellowish as it attains perfect maturity, and covered with a very thin bloom.

Pulp colour: pale rose-pink or light coppery colour with an opaline shimmer.

Description: Fruit, very small, oblate, marked with longitudinal ridges. Eye, open like an eyelet-hole. Stalk, one-eighth of an inch long. Flesh; dry, coarse, and not at all well-flavoured.

Breba Crop: unknown.

Listed by George Neilson in 1874 as being grown at the RVHS gardens at Burnley. Now Lost.

 Desert King

Synonyms: Charlie; King.

Provenance: A San Pedro type fig originally introduced in 1930 from Madera California.

Skin colour: Deep green, minutely spotted white.

Pulp colour: Strawberry red.

Description: The fruit is large and pyriform, the flesh is sweet. Delicious fresh or dried.

Breba Crop: unknown

Other information: Needs to be pollinated (caprified), to have good fruit set. The tree is vigorous, hardy and does well in cool areas, even growing in coastal British Columbia.

Sources (as of publication date): Commercially available in the U.S.A. but no known sources in Australia.

De St. Jeane

Grown at Burnley in Victoria during the 19th century. Whereabouts unknown. This is possibly a misspelling of the popular French cultivar Grise de la Saint Jean, also unavailable in Australia.

De Quatre Saisons

Has been misspelled as 'De Quartre Saissons.' The name translates from the French as 'Four Seasons'. Grown at Burnley in Victoria during the 19th century. Whereabouts unknown. No description.

Don's Drying

From Tony Stevens' collection. Probably named by Tony and probably good for drying. Currently growing in private Australian collections. Nothing else is known.

Don's Early

From Tony Stevens' collection. Like 'Don's Drying', probably named by Tony in honour of the person from whom he obtained it. Currently growing in private Australian collections. Nothing else is known.

D' Or de Laura

Hogg (1884) writes: 'Fruit, below medium size, oblong, marked with obscure ribs. Skin, green, becoming yellowish or dirty white when fully ripe. Eye, closed. Flesh, opaline, very tender and melting, rich, sugary, and delicious. Dries and shrivels well.'

Lost in Australia.

DORÉE

Synonyms: Figue d'Or (Golden Fig), Goutte d'Or, Doree.

Provenance: Originally from Provence in France, first described in 1667.

Skin colour: Yellowish green to rose-pink.

Pulp colour: Light rose.

Description: Main-crop figs smaller than brebas, globe-shaped, or shaped like squat pears; stalk swollen; no ribs; colour yellow to rose, pulp pale rose-pink. A good quality fig, excellent for drying.

Breba Crop: Trees of Dorée produce two crops. Brebas large, elongated-pyriform, somewhat oblique; average weight 85 grams; neck not distinct, merging gradually with the body; stalk conical, swollen toward the junction with the fruit, about 1/2 inch long; ribs not very well marked; eye in a slight depression, large, half open; scales erect, yellow to rose-coloured; skin delicate, yellowish green, becoming golden yellow slightly tinged with rose on the exposed side; pulp salmon; texture fine; seeds few; quality fair.

Other information: Once grown at Burnley in Victoria. Dorée was reported by early writers (17th, 18th, 19th century) to be subject to splitting or cracking of the skin, and therefore good only for hog feed; the checked skin also suggested to them the torn robe of a beggar; in general, however, it is described as a handsome fig of excellent quality.

Whereabouts unknown.

DOTTATO

Dottato is another name for Kadota. See Kadota.

Dr. Hogg's Black

Provenance: Hogg (1884) writes, 'I introduced this variety in 1864, having met with it in a vineyard near Toulouse. It was sent to the garden of the Royal Horticultural Society at Chiswick, and as no name accompanied it, it became distinguished as "Dr. Hogg's Black." I have not yet been able to identify it with any other variety; but there is no doubt that as we become better acquainted with the figs grown in the south of France and in Spain the correct name will some day be discovered.

Skin colour: Dark Mulberry

Pulp colour: Dull red

Description: Fruit, about medium size, oblong obovate. Neck, very short or wanting. Skin, slightly hairy, of a dark mulberry colour, covered with a thick bloom, and numerous little white specks on the surface, which is slightly furrowed in longitudinal lines, and the skin cracks lengthwise when the fruit is fully ripe. Stalk, very short and thick. Eye, small and closed. Flesh, dull red, with a thick syrupy juice, very richly flavoured.

Other information: Grown at Burnley in Victoria during the 19th century. Whereabouts unknown.

Dwarf Prolific

Grown at Burnley in Victoria during the 19th century. Whereabouts unknown.

 Early Violet

Synonyms: Early Violette

Provenance: Listed by John J Cole in 1867

Skin colour: Chocolate-brown.

Pulp colour: Strawberry.

Description: The main crop is small, turbinate to oblate-spherical, fair to good quality, subject to spoilage.

Breba Crop: None.

Other information: Recorded as having been grown at Burnley. Facciola (1990) describes Early Violet as a small-fruited variety with brownish red skin and red flesh of good flavour. 'Much too small to cultivate except for variety.' Early Violet was grown in the 19th. century in the UK as a greenhouse variety.

Hogg writes: 'Small, roundish. Skin, brownish red, covered with blue bloom. Flesh; red and well-flavoured. Tree hardy, and an abundant bearer... Though small, and in the estimation of some an insignificant variety, this is [preeminent] among figs — nicely flavoured, very early, and remarkably prolific.'

Whereabouts unknown in Australia. Available from Davis California, U.S.A.

 Eileen Wilde

From Tony Stevens' collection. Probably named by Tony in honour of the person from whom he obtained it. Currently growing in private Australian collections. Nothing else is known.

 Esperance Heritage

This cultivar was collected by a private grower in Western Australia. It is probably named after the Shire of Esperance. Currently growing in private collections. No other information can be found.

 Excel

Synonyms: Yellow Excel, Kadota Hybrid, Dottato Hybrid.

Provenance: Bred by Ira Condit at Riverside, California. A Condit hybrid, using Kadota as the mother, named and released by W. B. 'Bill' Storey in 1975. Hart lists 'Excel' as growing at Hillside Farm, W.A., in 2001.

Skin colour: Yellow

Pulp colour: Light amber

Description: Small to medium, early season fig. Oblate to spherical. Fruit has no neck, is blocky, very sweet and does not split. Figs are sweeter and have a smaller eye than its ancestor Kadota. Excellent, all-purpose fig, outstanding flavour, excellent as fresh fruit, canning or drying,

Breba Crop: Light breba crop

Other information: The tree is early bearing and vigorous. Leaf: base truncate to subcordate; three lobes; shallow sinuses.

Sources (as of publication date): Was trialed at Narara Arboretum, in N.S.W. and is now sold by Daleys Nursery in Kyogle in N.S.W. It is, by their account, well-adapted to subtropical conditions in Australia. Also sold by Yalca and Food Forest.

 Felice

This cultivar is provisionally named, and may turn out to be Black Portugal or Mission. The grower is waiting for it to fruit. Described as a 'huge, black fig' by the Australian of Italian descent who provided cuttings.

 Ficarra

This cultivar is provisionally named while the grower is waiting for it to fruit. The scion donor, of Italian descent, described it as a 'naturally dwarfing plant bearing small, red-pulped very sweet fruit'. The fruit is often eaten stuffed with a single blanched almond and lightly barbecued.

 Fiesta di Desire

A selection from Steve Karapetis, a nurseryman in Darwin, NT. From Tony Stevens' collection. Now grown by private growers.

 Figue d'Or

Listed as growing at Burnley, Victoria, in 1896. Whereabouts now unknown. See Dorée and Angélique Noir.

 FLANDERS

Synonyms: Verdone Hybrid. See Conadria.

Provenance: Bred from a seedling of White Adriatic and released by Ira Condit in 1975. One of Dr. Condit's varieties which came out of the breeding program at Riverside, California and were selected on the basis of being crack- and split-resistant; most have a small eye. All have very high sugar content and are very resistant to decay.

Conflicts: There exist two differing descriptions for this fruit. Version 1: Skin colour is greenish-yellow to brownish yellow with violet stripes, pulp colour is amber. Exceptionally beautiful fruits, elongated to the extent they hang like tear-drops. Medium sized, pyriform fruit with long slender neck, skin light tawny with longitudinal violet stripes and white flecks, pulp light strawberry. Version 2: Skin colour is green and pulp colour is pink.

Browsing through photos of Flanders figs on American websites brings up a few images of purple stripes figs and numerous pictures of figs with green skin and pink flesh. Given that Flanders is descended from the green-skinned White Adriatic, it would seem more likely that it is green-skinned itself. Perhaps there are two cultivars with the same name.

More information: Trees are vigorous but not particularly hardy. Widely adapted, producing well in both cool and hot regions, though best suited to warm climates. Fruit ripens mid to late season. Very firm when ripe, with strong, superb, sweet, rich flavour.

Sources (as of publication date): In Tony Stevens' collection. Currently available from Graham Brookman at the Food Forest, Gawler, South Australia. He describes the Flanders variety he offers as having 'green skin and pink flesh'.

Florentine

Synonyms: Italian Honey (see Italian Honey).
Provenance: Italy
Skin colour: Green
Pulp colour: Honey-coloured
Description: Sweet flavoured.
Breba Crop:
Other information: Grown as a container variety in the Eastern states of the U.S.A. If this is the same as Italian Honey Fig, then it is currently grown in Australia.
Sources (as of publication date): Private growers.

Genoa, Black

Synonyms: Nigra, Negro d'Espagne, Noire de Languedoc, Black Geneva.
Conflicts: San Piero, San Pedro.
Provenance: Hogg (1884) writes: This is the large black fig so extensively grown in Languedoc and Provence.
Skin colour: Dark purple, almost black and covered with a thick blue bloom.
Pulp colour: Yellowish under the skin, but dark red towards the interior.
Description: Long, conical, obovate fruit, medium sized. Juicy, with an excellent, sweet and very rich flavour. Ripens early in summer. May not be suitable for drying.
Breba Crop: One of the highest yielding varieties that will bear two crops a year in most climates.
Other information: This is the leading commercial variety for fresh fruit production in N.S.W. The tree has an open and spreading habit. The fruit is best suited for fresh eating. This is a very vigorous, hardy and productive variety that is often seen growing commercially due to its high yields.

The Black Genoa matures slightly earlier than Brown Turkey. Trees are reliable and popular for home gardens. This fig needs to be pollinated to set good crops of fruit. According to Ikin in the N.S.W. & Victorian state fruit collections in 1974.

Sources (as of publication date): Offered by Goodman's in 1903 catalogue and still offered for sale by Daleys Nursery, the Diggers' Club, Garden Express, Incredible Edibles, Ellenby Tree Farm and Blerick Fruit Trees.

Ficus carica 'Black Genoa'

 GENOA, LARGE BLACK

Goodmans Fruit Catalogue of 1911. Still offered by Goodmans in their 1988 catalogue. Listed by Ikin in the Queensland state fruit collection in 1974. No description, but presumably looks like Black Genoa only bigger.

Whereabouts unknown.

Genoa, Large White

Round large, obovate fruit with thin pale yellow skin. The flesh is and well flavoured. Listed by Ikin in the Victorian & Western Australian state fruit collections in 1974. Whereabouts are now unknown.

Genoa, White

Synonyms: Blanche; Figue Blanche; Ford's Seedling; Genoa; Lattarula; Lemon; Marseilles; White Geneva; White Marseilles; White Naples. Facciola distinguishes between White Genoa and White Marseilles.

Provenance: A heritage cultivar from Italy. Listed in Railton's catalogue in 1880 and Goodman's catalogue in 1914.

Skin colour: Green to greenish-yellow mottled with white.

Pulp colour: Amber to reddish-pink.

Description: A uniquely flavoured, tender fig with sweet flesh and few seeds. White Genoa has a milder flavour, not quite as rich for those who don't like the really intense fig flavour. Some describe it as a lemony flavour. Ripens mid-season. Medium to large in size, pyriform. Good for eating fresh, drying, preserving or making jam.

Breba Crop: Light crop in December. Brebas are oblique-pyriform; with light strawberry pulp, hollow at the centre.

Main crop in February — March (Australia). Main crop are turbinate.

Other information: Does not produce heavy crops of either brebas or main crop figs. Seems to be a better performer than others in cooler areas. Does not do well in hotter climates, where Conadria is a far better choice. Genoa needs annual pruning. Self-fruitful

Sources (as of publication date): White Genoa was growing at Burnley, Victoria, in 1896. It is still common in cultivation and is offered commercially by Yalca, Daleys, Tass 1 Trees, Newman's Nursery and Old Farm Nursery (Wholesalers).

 Good

Ficus carica 'Good' was listed by Hart as being grown at at Gosnells Hillside Farm in 2001. Tony Stevens had a specimen of Good growing in his collection. Currently it is growing in private fig collections.

Gourande Rouge

Mentioned in 'Benson's guide to fig culture in the open ground at the North' (1886) but with no description.

Hogg (1884) describes its sister fig Gourande Noir: 'Fruit, about medium size, oblong. Skin, quite black. Flesh, deep red, and deliciously flavoured. A very excellent fig, which is much grown in Languedoc, and where I have eaten it from the tree in great perfection.'

Listed in Goodman's catalogue of 1909. Lost.

Gourandi

Grown by the RHSV in the 1890s at Burnley. Lost.

Grossale

Grossale is a synonym of the Italian fig Grossagna. Other synonyms of this fig include Grossagne and Grossales. This heritage fruit was grown by the RHSV in the 1890s at Burnley. Now lost. Mentioned in 'Benson's guide to fig culture in the open ground at the North' (1886) but with no description.

Grosse Blanche De Marseilles

Grown by the RHSV in the 1890s at Burnley. Now lost.

Grosse Monstrueuse

A synonym of Grosse Monstrueuse De Lipari.

Grosse Monstrueuse De Lipari

Synonyms: Grosse Monstreuse. Sometimes misspelled as Grosse Monstreuse De Lipari. See also De Lipari.

Lipari is an Italian island of the coast of Sicily.

Bill Hankin writes, 'Listed in the report by George Neilson for the RVHS gardens at Burnley in 1875. Offered by W C Grey in 1907. Described as having very large fruit with brown skin and red flesh of good flavour. There is a wax replica fig called 'Grosse Monstrueuse' at the Science Works Museum in Victoria. A variety called simply 'Monstreuse' is also available from Davis California, U.S.A. and this may be the same.'

Hogg (1884) describes it as 'Fruit, very large; three inches wide and nearly as much high; turbinate and broad and flattened at the apex. Skin, pale chestnut brown, darker on the side exposed to the sun, and marked with darker longitudinal ribs down the sides, and with occasional dark spots, the whole surface covered with a thick bloom. Stalk, short and thick. Eye, large and closed. Flesh, dull red, thick, juicy, and well-flavoured. A large and handsome fig of great merit, which I found in an orchard in the department of Bouches de Rhone, and introduced to the Royal Horticultural Society. The tree is a good grower and bears abundantly.'

Sources: 'Monstreuse' is sold commercially in the U.S.A., but Grosse Monstrueuse De Lipari is lost in Australia.

Grosse Rouge De Bordeaux

Grosse Rouge De Bordeaux is a synonym for San Piero, which in turn is a synonym for Black Genoa. This does not mean that these figs are identical, because 'San Piero' is used as a synonym for many figs. It only emphasises the vast amount of confusion associated with fig names.

Grown at Burnley in Victoria during the 19th century. Whereabouts now unknown.

Grosse Verte

Listed in the report by George Neilson for the RVHS gardens at Burnley in 1875. 'Large yellowish green skinned fruit with red flesh; very late': Goodman's Fruit Catalogue of 1921. Railton's catalogue of 1880 states that this variety ripens in February in Victoria.

Hogg (1884) writes that Grosse Verte is merely a synonym for Nebian. He describes Nebian as 'Fruit, above medium size, roundish ovate, and marked with obscure longitudinal ribs. Skin, quite green, a bright pea green, becoming a little yellow at maturity, and not covered with any bloom. Stalk, a quarter of an inch long. Eye, open. Flesh, very dark red throughout, and firm, with a rich and sugary flavour. Rather late [ripening]. Condit, on the other hand, reports that Grosse Verte is merely a synonym of Verdone, as is 'White Adriatic'.

Sources: White Adriatic is available from most nurseries.

Harold Jo

Collected by Tony Stevens and named in honour of the married couple who gave him the cuttings. The fruit is small, soft delicious; a bit bigger than Celeste, more delicate.

Source: Growing in private collections.

Hasbargen Brown

Cuttings of this cultivar were given to a grower in Western Australia. Nothing else is known about it.

Hill's Large Brown

Grown by the RHSV in the 1890s at Burnley. Lost

 Hollis Purple

Provenance: Neil Barraclough of Gippsland writes in 2013, 'The following figs were saved from either Bathurst or Orange research stations (NSW) when they were being removed a bit over twenty years ago. I grew out the cuttings and gave them to a mate (Peter) who still has them. Unfortunately he used the aluminium from blue Foster's beer cans to label them, and bower birds pinched some of the blue labels.'

Fortunately Hollis Purple retained its label. Barraclough describes it as having 'good fruit'.

Sources: growing in private Australian collections.

Hollis White

Provenance - see Hollis Purple. Neil Barraclough describes the fruit of Hollis White as not particularly good, but adds, 'Hollis White has the potential to be a good dwarfing rootstock.'

Sources: growing in private Australian collections.

Honey - see Celeste
Honey, Italian - See Italian Honey

Rare and Heritage Fig Cultivars

in Australia
I to N

ISCHIA

Ischia is a volcanic island in Italy; doubtless the source of this cultivar. We know that Ischia grew in Australia in the 19th century. From an article in the newspaper, *South Australian Register* 1890. 'The best varieties in Victoria for drying ... were the Smyrna, the Ischia, and the White Genoa.'

Four colours of Ischia still exist in Australia, but Ischia itself seems to be lost.

ISCHIA, BLACK

Synonyms: Black Ishi; Black Provence; Blue Ischia; Nero; Ischia Black; Early Forcing; Ronde Noire.

Skin colour: Dark purple, almost black.

Provenance: An Italian cultivar. Named after the Mediterranean island of Ischia, off the coast of Naples, where this variety originated. Offered by John C. Cole in 1867.

Pulp colour: Strawberry pink to deep red.

Description: A small to medium sized turbinate fruit, flattened at the top. Very soft skin and flesh. An outstanding flavour, sweet, rich and luscious. Main crop is elongated pear shaped with many noticeable ribs; short neck and short to medium stalk; large, 2 1/2 in (6.35 cm) long and 1 1/2 in (3.8 cm) wide; dark purple-black except at the apex where it is lighter and greenish; there are many golden flecks; skin is wholly coated with thin, dark-blue bloom; eye open, with red-violet scales; pulp is violet-red, of good quality.

Breba Crop: In the breba crop, there are few ribs and mostly indistinct; the fruit is small, about 1 1/2 in (3.8 cm) long and of the same width at the apex; the pulp is red to greenish-amber; of poor flavour.

Other information: The tree is not particularly hardy. One of the joys of growing figs is being able to eat them fresh, and this is an excellent variety to be able to pick directly from the tree. Because of its soft skin it is very difficult for growers to get them to a commercial outlet in good condition. As a backyard tree though, it is wonderful variety.

The tree is particularly ornamental, with red buds, and the leaves are glossy, only shallowly three-lobed. A heavy bearer, ripening a little after Black Genoa. Offered by Goodman's Fruit Catalogue of 1900.Offered by W. C. Grey in 1907. Listed by Ikin in the N.S.W. and Victorian state fruit collections in 1974. James Railton's catalogue of the 1880's states that this variety ripens in the second week of January in Victoria. (Australia)

Black Ischia was grown at Burnley, Victoria, in 1896.

Sources (as of publication date): In Tony Stevens' collection. Currently being grown privately.

Ficus carica 'Black Ischia'. Image: Trees of Joy.

ISCHIA, BROWN

Mentioned in the *Australian Town and Country Journal* in 1892 as being offered for sale by the Universal Nursery Company, Wahroonga, N.S.W. Currently found only in a single private collection in Gippsland, Victoria.

 Ischia, Green

Synonyms: Verte

Provenance: An Italian cultivar. Named after the Mediterranean island of Ischia, off the coast of Naples, where this variety originated.

Skin colour: Greenish yellow.

Pulp colour: Strawberry pink.

Description: Small fig with an excellent flavour. Excellent fresh or dried.

Breba Crop: Good breba crop.

Other information: Small tree. Recommended for short summer climates.

Sources (as of publication date): In Tony Stevens' collection. Being grown privately.

 Ischia, Yellow

Synonyms: Yellow Ischi, White Ischia

Provenance: An Italian cultivar. Named after the Mediterranean island of Ischia, off the coast of Naples, where this variety originated. Offered in Australia by John J. Cole in his 1867 catalogue. Offered by W. C. Grey in 1907.

Skin colour: pale greenish yellow.

Description: The fruit is rich and sugary. Flavour is very rich and luscious. Small, good for preserving whole or making jam.

Breba Crop: unknown.

Other information: A great bearer with the second crop heaviest. Confused description but probably meant that it had large fruit with yellow skin and red flesh.

Sources (as of publication date): In Tony Stevens' collection. Being grown privately. Possibly available from the Food Forest in South Australia.

 ISCHIA, WHITE

Provenance: Another Italian cultivar from Ischia.

Skin colour: green

Pulp colour: strawberry

Description: Small green fruit, strawberry pulp. Grown in pots in the UK. Still common in cultivation (Lord 1957). Facciola's (1990) description is similar to Green Ischia except that this one 'ripens early'. Grown in Burnley, Victoria, in 1896.

 ITALIAN HONEY

Synonyms: Figo Bianco, Blanche, Lemon, White Marseille, White Marseilles, Italian Golden, Honey Fig. See also Florentine and La Royale.

Conflicts: Lattarula, Florentine.

Provenance: Italy. Hart lists this cultivar as growing at Hillside Farm, W.A., in 2001.

Skin colour: Greenish to golden.

Pulp colour: Ivory-cream to honey-amber.

Description: Medium to large fruit with very sweet lemony flavour

Breba Crop: Yes, a light breba crop.

Other information: Makes an excellent container plant. Valuable in short-season, cool-summer areas. Slow growing, dense, hardy tree.

Sources (as of publication date): Being grown privately.

 Jenny Smith Blue

Synonyms: None known.
Provenance: Unknown.
Skin colour: Purple to blue.
Pulp colour: Pink/ red.
Description: Medium to large fruit.
Breba Crop: unknown.
Other information: Jenny Smith Blue is a hardy, spreading medium sized deciduous tree. Fruit ripens mid season. The tree is self-fertile. A fantastic fig for cooking. The tree is a heavy bearer.
Sources (as of publication date): Olea Wholesale Nurseries in Western Australia.

 Jerusalem

Synonyms: Figue Goutte, Gerusalem, De Gerusalem, Di Gerusaleme, De Jerusalem.
Provenance: France. First described by Audibert Frères (1854).
Skin colour: Green, shaded with brown or violet?
Pulp colour: Strawberry pink?
Description: Fruit is medium in size, up to 1-7/8 inches in diameter and 1-1/2 inches in length, oblate spherical, mostly without neck; average weight 39 grams; stalk short and thick; ribs fairly prominent; eye medium to large, open, with violet scales; white flecks scattered. Caprified specimens are darker-coloured on the outside and of a deeper strawberry inside than when uncaprified; quality good to very good; skin colour unattractive.
Breba Crop: None.
Other information: The tree drops its fruit badly unless caprification is practiced. It is a poor bearer.
Condit calls Jerusalem 'A variety of no particular value.' Nonetheless. it is possible that the tree grown by Condit in

California as Jerusalem was another cultivar entirely. There is much disagreement about skin colour in the literature.[1]

Generally, cultivars with many synonyms are those which are popular, and Jerusalem has at least four. Furthermore, Eisen describes Jerusalem as 'Medium, roundish; stalk stout and short. Eye quite closed; skin black, with reddish mahogany toward the stalk; blue bloom. Pulp dark blood red, rich, sweet, and finely flavoured. A very good fig.'

The original Jerusalem must have had high value, because it was grown by the RHSV in the 1890's at Burnley and listed by Ikin in the Queensland state fruit collection in 1974, though it is now lost.

 JERUSALEM, PINK

Provenance: Hart lists Pink Jerusalem as growing at Hillside Farm, W.A., in 2001. Cuttings of this cultivar were later acquired by a grower in W.A. and passed on to Victorian growers.

Skin colour: Green.

Pulp colour: Pale golden-green.

Description: Excellent flavour, very sweet, medium size, oblate..

Other information: A vigorous tree.

Sources: Growing in private collections.

---

1   Condit writes: 'The main disagreement in the descriptions concerns fruit colour, which Hogg and Eisen give as black, while Audibert Frères and La Brousse term the colour brown. On the other hand, Société' Pomologique de France and Delbard give the skin colour as light or yellowish.'

 Kadota

Synonyms: White Kadota, Dottato, Florentine, Honey, Gentile, Dattero, White Endich.

Provenance: The most common green type, the Kadota is believed to be thousands of years old. Pliny the Elder is said to have commended this variety, known in Italy as the Dotatto.

Skin colour: Pale yellowish-green to clear yellow/creamy amber.

Pulp colour: Amber.

Description: Small to medium sized pyriform fruit. Delicious fresh or dried. Pulp is particularly smooth and silky. It is a rich, sweet, all-purpose fig and the most common canned fig. The sweetest yellow fig. Skin tough. Nearly seedless. Used for canning commercially, drying or eating fresh. Also good for preserves. Forms 'honey drop' at eye. The eye is open but it is characteristically filled with a honey-like substance which prevents entry of insects and subsequent souring. A very high quality fig.

Breba Crop: Has a few very large early figs followed by a main crop. When pruned moderately will produce both first and second crops. Tend to over-bear and produce under-sized fruit unless moderately pruned annually.

Other information: The tree is vigorous and productive. Fairly hardy. Fruit needs warm weather to ripen. Good for hot climates. Long lived adaptable tree. Requires heat to develop its best flavour and texture. Self-fruitful.

This variety is the commercial fig of California. The fruit becomes rubbery in drier and hotter areas. It will produce on suckerwood the year after frost injury.

Sources (as of publication date): From Tony Stevens' collection; now in the collections of private growers.

 ## King

Synonyms: Charlie, Desert King, White King.
Provenance: Originated in California about 1920.
Skin colour: Greenish yellow.
Pulp colour: Strawberry pink.
Description: A high quality fig, medium to large, pyriform to oblique. Sweet and rich. Excellent fresh or dried.
Breba Crop: Large.
Other information: Well-adapted to growing in a cool climate. A San Pedro type, it sometimes sets main crop figs without pollination. Fairly hardy. Prune only lightly, occasionally. (Heavy winter pruning removes breba crop.) Main crop is light in hot climates, heavier in coastal climates.
Sources (as of publication date): From Tony Stevens' collection; now in the collections of private growers.

 ## Kungasava Strawberry

Provenance: collected by a private W.A grower who says it 'tastes like strawberry'. Possibly White Adriatic by another name?

 ## Large Blue

'Large Blue' was offered by John J Cole in 1860s. Tree has large leaves and is handsome. Fruit is 'above medium size with bluish purple skin and purple flesh, but not richly flavoured.' Listed in the Report by George Neilson for the RVHS gardens at Burnley in 1875.

This fruit may possibly be confused with 'Italian Large Blue', which is a synonym of 'Brown Turkey'. See Brown Turkey.

 La Royale

We can find nothing in the literature about 'La Royale', however 'Royale' is a synonym of Blanche. See also 'Italian Honey Fig'.

Listed in Australia in Goodman's Fruit Catalogue of 1909 to 1911. Sold by Law Sumner in 1915. No description. Lost.

Lemon Lennie

Provenance: Collected by Tony Stevens. According to John Rance, the members of the Rare Fruit South Australia committee named this fig after one of the committee members, Lennie Bosch.

Description: The fruit has a lemon tang.

Source: Growing in private collections.

Lisbon

Collected by a grower in W.A. and possibly originating from the Stoneville Research Station. Nothing else known.

Longue Blanche de Provence

Listed in the Report by George Neilson for the RVHS gardens at Burnley in 1875. Not mentioned elsewhere

Lop Ingir

Synonyms: Lop, Green Packing Fig, Lob Ingir.

See also 'Calimyrna'.

Western Mail, Perth, W.A. Saturday 29 June 1912: '[There are] probably hundreds of varieties of figs grown in Turkey in Asia. Out of this large number probably about twenty are considered especially valuable.

'Many years ago what are considered the most valuable varieties were introduced into... South Australia and Victoria. More recently they have been' introduced into this State. The most valuable of all ls the Lop or green packing fig, known as Lop Ingir or Lob Ingir, and next to that the Sar Lop or yellow packing fig. Ingir is, I believe, Turkish for fig. It is from these two varieties that the finest quality dried figs are made.' Lost.

 MACKENWOOD

Grown by the RHSV in the 1890s at Burnley. Lost

 MADELINE

Condit writes: 'Madeline: Variety received in 1923 from a grower at San Jose, California. Produced medium-sized figs, dark violet in colour, with strawberry pulp. The Madeline described by Earle (1900) is probably Blanche (Madeleine). Identity of Madeline not determined.'

See also Italian Honey Fig.

Railton's catalogue of 1880s states that this variety has small pale yellow fruit that are very rich, ripening at the end of December in Victoria. Grown by the RHSV in the 1890s at Burnley. Goodman's Fruit Catalogue of 1911 lists the variety but with .no description. Lost.

 MALTA

Synonyms: Small Brown.

Hogg writes in The Fruit Manual: 'Small, roundish turbinate, compressed at the apex. Skin, pale brown when fully ripe. Flesh, the same colour as the skin; very sweet and well-flavoured. If allowed to hang till it shrivels, it becomes quite a sweetmeat.'

Malta figs ripen late.

Described by Crichton as a 'a small, richly flavoured variety of doubtful origin suitable for drying. Tree fair, vigorous and bears freely.'

Malta was introduced into Australia by the RHSV in the 1880s. Now lost.

 Marseillaise

Synonyms: Marseilles.
Grown by the RHSV in the 1890s at Burnley. Lost

 Martin

Provenance: Martin Farm, Pedler Creek, South Australia.
Skin colour: Black
Pulp colour: Red
Description: A large black pyriform (shaped like a pear) fig with red clean juicy flesh.
Breba Crop: average, ripens late December.
Main crop: excellent, ripens early March.
Other information: Eye is medium sized and partly open. Very good for glacé and jam making.
Tree Sources: Privately grown by members of Rare Fruit South Australia

Martinique

Synonyms: Black Martinique
Provenance: France. Described by Ounous (1863). Grown at Riverside in California since 1931. Description is from figs produced at Riverside.

Skin colour: Purplish black
Pulp colour: Light strawberry to dark red.
Description: Main-crop figs below medium to small, up to 1-1/2 inches in length and the same in diameter; shape turbinate-spherical to pyriform, sometimes oblique; average weight 23 grams; neck distinct, generally somewhat flattened; stalk short; ribs prominent, conspicuous on account of deeper colouration than body; eye medium, open, surrounded by a zone of lighter colour, scales tinged with violet; surface dull, with fairly heavy bloom; white flecks scattered, of medium size and prominence; colour purplish black, with neck remaining green; solid; flavour rich and sweet, very good. Quality good as a fresh fruit; external colour poor when dried. Caprified

specimens, when mature, show checked skin and dark-strawberry pulp; flavour subacid.

Breba Crop: Breba figs are very few, or none

Other information: The tree is rather densely branched; terminal buds are brown. There is also a White Martinique and a Martinique,

Listed in the Report by George Neilson for the RVHS gardens at Burnley in 1875. Not mentioned elsewhere. Lost

Mary Lane

Synonyms: Mary Jane, Seedless, Jelly, Mary Jane Jelly.
Provenance: California
Skin colour: Green to yellow
Pulp colour: Yellow
Description: A medium to large yellow fig. This fig is virtually seedless. Yellow pulp is very juicy and sweet. It fills out well and has an excellent flavour. This is an outstanding, high quality fig with the exception that it will possibly split during adverse weather conditions. The tightly closed eye makes it resistant to spoiling.
Breba Crop: unknown
Other information: Well adapted to all fig growing areas. Trees are rampant growers, spreading to 15 feet. Great fresh, dried, or preserved. Mary Lane is self-pollinating and is very productive. A medium to average sized tree at maturity.
Tree sources (as of publication date): in Tony Stevens' collection and grown privately.

Ficus carica 'Mary Lane'.

 Minorca Bianca

Offered by W. C. Grey in Australia in 1907. described as having medium sized fruit with a green skin. Fine quality. Whereabouts unknown.

 Mission

Synonyms: Black Mission, Black California, California Black, Californian Large Black, California, Black Mexican, Franciscan, Franciscana, Francisciana, Beer's Black, Negra.

The following names have also been cited as synonyms[2]: Reculver, Brebal, Biberaeo, Gourreau diu Languedoc, Gourreau Noir, Noire d'Espagne, Gouraund Noir, Gourand Noir, Douro Nebra.

Conflicts: Violette de Bordeaux, Negronne.

Provenance: More than two centuries ago, in 1768, Franciscan missionaries voyaged from the Balearic Islands in Spain to San Diego in Southern California, U.S.A. They carried with them some cuttings from their favourite fig tree. Father Junipero Serra planted these cuttings at the San Diego mission settlement, and the cultivar became known as 'Mission'.

The Franciscans propagated this fig in the subsequent missions they established along the California coast. Gustav Eisen writes, "The early padres and missionaries in the Pacific coast States cultivated no other variety of fig".[3]

'It later became the main commercial variety planted throughout California.'[4]

---

[2]   *Fig Varieties: Hilgardia, Vol. 23, No. 11, 1955, p. 437, by Condit and The Fig in Georgia, Georgia Experiment Station, Bull. 61, 1903, p. 69, by Starnes.*
[3]   *The Fig: Its History, Culture, and Curing, by Gustav Eisen, published in 1901, page 255*
[4]   Wikipedia

Skin colour: Purple-black. 'Skin rough, slightly hairy or downy, deep mahogany violet with reddish flush in shade and on stalk covered with a thin bloom.'[5]

Pulp colour: Strawberry/watermelon pink. 'Pulp not fine, red. but not blooded, rather brownish-amber red, shaded dark amber; sweet, but not high-flavoured.'[6]

Description: A medium-sized to huge, sweet fig with a distinctive, rich flavour, sometimes called 'the taste standard for figs'. The shape is somewhat elongated and pear-like.

Mission is a cultivar of excellent quality and a very heavy bearer, with large breba and main crops. If grown in a suitable climate, it can produce all year round. Early ripening. Wikipedia reports that 'When the fruit is ripe, the skin frequently cracks'. Figs4Fun reports 'Fruit splitting is minimal, and the eye is fairly tight, so fruit spoilage is seldom a problem.'

Properly ripe Mission figs have a luscious, jammy texture. If allowed to dry out (like prunes) while still hanging on the tree, their texture becomes more chewy and the sweetness increases even more.

The tree commences growth midseason. Mission produces its leaves in spring about seven days after Adriatic. The base of the five-lobed leaf is spurred. The leaf is glossy, longer than broad and lighter green than most other figs, and most characteristically mottled with lighter, yellowish green. This is because Mission fig trees are usually infected with Fig Mosaic Virus, an incurable malaise which usually does not kill the tree, merely weakens it, makes the leaves appear speckled and may sometimes reduce fruit quantity.

The tree's lower branches droop, and its bark is light in colour. Very vigorous, but not hardy. Drought tolerant and self fertile. It lives for a very long time and eventually reaches a considerable size. Mission is frost-sensitive, but can easily

---

5   *Pacific Rural Press, Volume 53, Number 22, 29 May 1897*
6   *ibid*

be grown in Australian plant hardiness zones 3 and 4, which is roughly equivalent to USDA zone 9 and up. Very widely adapted variety grows and produces well in most regions. Suits the coast or inland. The most dependable, all-round backyard fig variety.

Ficus carica 'Mission'. Image: J. Marchini Farms

Light pruning only is recommended—enough to provide a uniform shape and encourage good fruit production. Heavier pruning may be done to control size. Do not prune the tree after it reaches maturity.

Not suitable for espalier.

Breba Crop: large

The breba, or 'first' crop ripens before most other varieties. It matures in late December, (June in the northern hemisphere).

Brebas are pyriform with a prominent thick neck; main crop figs are smaller and more variable, pyriform.

'First crop or brebas large to medium: long turbinate with the greatest diameter between the center and the apex, which is rounded, sometimes even pointed, causing the shape of the fig to become ovoid. Neck long, gradually set: stalk medium to short: ribs distinct, well-marked. Eye prominent, raised, open, but not very large; scales rosy.'7

The large breba fruits are suitable for shipping to the fresh market. Some are dried, but due to their shape the dried figs are generally used in manufacturing.

Main Crop: medium in size.

The second crop matures in February and March (August and September in the northern hemisphere).

The more numerous figs of the main crop are smaller and rounder.

Other information: Mission is great for eating fresh and is also a good fig for drying, canning or preserves.

The deep purple hue of the fresh fig darkens to an attractive, rich black when the fruit is dried, which makes it a decorative as well as a delicious addition to recipes. However, 'On account of the productive capacity of the trees, resistance of the fruit to spoilage, and excellent quality both fresh and dried, the [Mission] has long enjoyed an excellent reputation. The main objection to it commercially is the black skin colour, which practically prohibits use of the dried fruit in fig paste.'8

The oldest fig in the U.S.A. 'The Mission fig was, in later years, surpassed by the Sari Lopi fig (also known as Calimyrna) as the most popular commercial fig variety grown in California.'9 The Mission fig is very rare in Australia.

Sources (as of publication date): This fig was in Tony Stevens' collection. In Australia, cultivars exist only in the hands of private fig collectors.

---

7 *ibid*
8 *Figues du Monde, retrieved March 2014*
9 *The New Fig Booklet, by Ray Givan, with Fred Born, published in 2007, page 3*

 ## Monaco Blanche

Listed in the plant report by George Neilson for the RVHS gardens at Burnley in 1875. Variety called Monaco Bianco listed as growing at Burnley in 1896 is probably the same variety. Not mentioned elsewhere.

Lost.

 ## Monaco Bianco

Possibly the same as Monaco Blanche. 'Fruit, above medium size, round, and flattened, with somewhat of a neck, but very little, and with obscure ribs. Skin, green, becoming yellowish green when ripe, and with a very thin bloom. Eye, large. Stalk, very short. Flesh, dark red, juicy, brisk, and well-flavoured, but not richly so.

'Rather a coarse fig. It cracks and opens much at the eye. The skin also cracks much. It is not a first-rate variety in comparison with some of the others.'10

Listed as growing at Burnley in 1896. Lost.

 ## Mouissoune

Robert Hogg describes this fig as 'Fruit, below medium size, round, and inclining to oblate, marked with distinct ribs, running from the stalk to the apex. Skin, quite black-purple, covered with blue bloom. Stalk, very short. Eye, open, showing the red inside. Flesh, bright rose-colour throughout, very juicy and tender, rich, syrupy, and delicious.'

Listed in the report by George Neilson for the RVHS gardens at Burnley in 1875. Not mentioned elsewhere. Lost.

Nagronne - see Negronne

---

10 Robert Hogg, 'The-Fruit-Manual'

 NEGRONNE

Synonyms: Facciola 1990[11] lists Negronne's synonyms as Bordeaux and Violette de Bordeaux.

Conflicts: A fig cultivar called 'Nagronne' was listed as being grown at the RVHS gardens at Burnley, Victoria, in the 19th century. This spelling is likely to have been an error. 'Negronne' was also listed by George Neilson in 1874 as being grown at the RVHS gardens, but with no description.

Provenance: The name suggests this cultivar comes from Italy, where 'negrone' means 'black guy'.

Skin colour: purplish-black

Pulp colour: pith tinged violet, pulp strawberry.

Description: Small black fruit with rich, excellent tasting red pulp. Closed eye. Spherical/pyriform, obovate. Of good flavour fresh or dried. Considered by many the finest tasting fig.

Breba Crop: reasonable.

Main crop: small

Other information: Good for home planting, as tree is dwarfing. Needs protection in cold winter areas. Similar fruit to Mission, but hardier and a smaller size tree.

Sources: Still available in the U.S.A. No known source in Australia any more.

---

11   Cornucopia: A source book of edible plants. Kampong Publications (Vista, CA, U.S.A.).

Ficus carica 'Negronne'. Image: Wayside gardens.

 Negrone

Listed in Grey's 1907 catalogue as 'Large, black, excellent; medium [sized tree?].' Probably a spelling error; this may have been referring to 'Negronne' (see above).

 Negro Large

Listed in the plant report by George Neilson for the RVHS gardens at Burnley in 1875. Probably a misspelling of 'Negro Largo' (see below). Whereabouts unknown

 Negro Largo

Synonyms: Brown Turkey, Aubique Noire, San Piero.

Listed in the Brunnings of 1916.

This *might* be the same as Brown Turkey, which is still grown in Australia. For details, see Turkey, Brown.

Negro De Espagne

Synonyms: Black Spanish, Brown Turkey ?

Listed in the plant report by George Neilson for the RVHS gardens at Burnley in 1875.

Whereabouts unknown

Nepolitaine

Listed in the plant report by George Neilson for the RVHS gardens at Burnley in 1875. This is very likely to be a misspelling of 'Napolitaine' (syns. Napolitano, Neapolitan), a cultivar from southern France. Eisen describes Napolitain as having a 'second crop; ripens in September, used fresh and dry. At Aix and Salon.'

The tree is said to be vigorous, and very productive.

The following description is from Société Pomologique de France; 'Brebas large; elongated oval; colour green, suffused with violet-bronze; pulp red; quality fair. Second-crop figs medium, turbinate; skin colour same as brebas; pulp red, sweet; quality very good.'

Whereabouts unknown.

 Nigra

Listed in the plant report by George Neilson for the RVHS gardens at Burnley in 1875.

Whereabouts unknown

Rare and Heritage Fig Cultivars

in Australia
O to S

 Osborne Prolific

Synonyms: Osborne's Prolific, Neveralla, Archipel, Archipal, Hardy Prolific, Osborn, Rust, Osborne.

Note: This fig may be the same as Archipal.

Provenance: 'An excellent fig, introduced [to Great Britain] by Messrs. Osborn, of the Fulham Nursery, in 1879. The tree is an abundant bearer, and is well adapted for pot culture.'[1] 'Osborne's Prolific' was listed in the Brunnings catalogue of 1916.

Skin colour: dark bronze/reddish mahogany, tinged with violet.

Pulp colour: amber/opaline tinged pale strawberry

Description: Medium to large sized. Fruit, roundish turbinate, tapering into a very long neck, some specimens measuring as much as three inches and three-quarters long from the eye to the end of the stalk. Skin, dark mahogany, gradually shading off to pale brown towards the neck, which is bright pea-green; the surface is thickly dotted and speckled with grey or white. Flesh, quite opaline, without any trace of red, with a rich, very sweet, syrupy juice and excellent flavour.[2] Early ripening.

Breba Crop: Good.

Main Crop: Main crop figs are pyriform with variable necks. Long slender stalks, to 2cm (1 inch) long.

Other information: The tree is slow growing but hardy and bears fruit heavily. Well-adapted in all fig growing areas. Trees ripen fruit even in cool weather. Naturally dwarf tree, good for container growing.

---

1   Robert Hogg: *The Fruit Manual*
2   ibid.

 Owen Special

This fig was collected in Western Australia and is growing in private collections. Nothing else is known.

 Oblique Blanche

Listed in Goodman's Fruit Catalogue of 1909 to 1914. No description, but judging by the name, it is of French origin and the skin was probably quite pale. Now lost.

 Oeil De Perdrix

The name translates from French as 'Eye of the Partridge'. Listed by George Neilson in 1874 as being grown at the RVHS gardens at Burnley. Still being grown there in 1896. No description was included in the catalogue.

In ornamental art, 'Oeil De Perdrix' means 'decorated with small round points, spots, or rings.'. The term can also mean 'having a brownish red colour'.

Now lost in Australia.

 Palane

Listed in the Report by George Neilson for the RVHS gardens at Burnley in 1874 . Still being grown there in 1896. Listed in Goodman's Fruit Catalogues of 1909 to 1914. No description. Now lost.

 # Panachée

Synonyms: Striped Tiger, Tiger, Striped Signora, Panachie, Panache, Variegato, Jaspee Limone, Marbled Limone, Plume, Figa Turca, Maravilla, Princessa, Rayonne, Courgette, Rayée, Jaspée, Bourjassotte, Père Hilarion, Zigarella, Col di Signora, Variegato, Fracazzano, Rigato, Bracotedesco, Ficus carica radiata, Risso, Ficus pachycarpa var. fasciata, Gasparrini, Tina ta Spanja.

Provenance: According to Condit (1928), the origin of this sectorial chimera (see appendix) is unknown. Karp writes, 'The variety was first described by that name, which means "variegated," in France in 1826, but similar types were noted as far back as the 17th century." Barron (1869) described Panachée as a sport from the better - known Col di Signora Bianca, one of the finest Italian varieties. Borg reported that a variegated fig, "Tina ta Spanja," grown at Marsascala in Malta, was said to be of Spanish origin, and needed caprification. Hart reported in 2001 that Panachée was growing at Hillside Farm in W.A. He added, 'Stock originally derived from importations from U.S.A. via N.S.W.'

Skin colour: Hogg describes it as 'Straw yellow, beautifully striped with longitudinal bands of bright, lively green, some of which are broad, others narrow.'

Pulp colour: 'Bright rose-colour throughout, with a thick rim of white skin as a margin to it.' (Hogg)

Description: Fruit is small to medium, texture is dry but flavour is sweet. Best fresh. Sweetest and most delicious when picked very ripe. Hogg writes that it is 'richly flavoured.' David Karp of the L.A. Times reports, 'Ripe specimens have super-sweet, jam-like pulp, with a counterbalancing acidity uncommon in other varieties and an intense berry flavour.' This cultivar has a relatively thick skin, which means it has a good shelf life. Requires long, warm growing season. Ripens late.

Breba Crop: No breba crop.

Main crop: Condit writes: 'Figs are medium, up to 6 cm (2 - 1/4 inches) in length and 5 cm (2 inches) in diameter; average weight 40 grams; shape pyriform, with neck prominent, and somewhat flattened in some specimens; stalk to 1 cm (3/8 inch) long; ribs practically absent; surface glossy, with a delicate bloom; white flecks inconspicuous; eye medium or above, open, scales variable, from chaffy to light violet; colour light yellow, with alternate bands of green, the latter fading out at complete maturity; meat thick, white pulp strawberry, mealy in texture; quality mediocre to poor. Caprified figs are somewhat larger, with pulp blood-red in colour. Splitting of fruit bad, even when uncaprified.'

Other information: The tree is moderately vigorous and upright in habit of growth. Tree is not very productive and fruit is not suitable for drying. This fig is arguably the most beautiful of all.

Tree Sources (as of publication date): Available commercially in the U.S.A. and grown in private Australian collections.

Ficus carica 'Panachée'

 Paradise

Paradise is a fig in the collection of Tony Stevens. It was given to him by Andrew Thompson, who named it after a northeastern suburb of Adelaide which is bounded on the north side by the River Torrens, in South Australia.

The fig is growing in private collections and no other information is known.

Peau Dure

Synonyms: Peldure

Provenance: Listed only by Crichton in 1893. The name is French, and translates as 'Rough Skin'.

Skin colour: pale yellowish green

Pulp colour: pale red

Description: A French variety. Fruit is medium sized, pyriform, with a short neck. Sweet, firm and rich."

Breba Crop: Medium-sized brebas are brown flushed with olive green and have reddish pulp. Very good with agreeable acidic undertones.

Main crop: Smaller main crop figs are olive tinged with violet. Resist rain damage and are excellent for drying.

Now lost in Australia.

 Persian Prolific

Provenance: Iran?

Skin colour: Light purple

Flesh Colour: Honey

Description: mid season fruit.

Breba Crop: unknown

Other information: The tree is a strong grower,

Sources: Food Forest.

 Peter Good

Provenance: Selected and named by W.A.N.A.T.C.A.[3] founder and president David Noel, who named it after 19th century botanist Peter Good. For more about Peter Good the man, see appendix.

Picone

Synonyms: Piconi
Skin colour: green
Pulp colour: dark red.
Provenance and description: Daleys Nursery in New South Wales reports: 'A favourite of local fruit enthusiast John Picone. This fig produces small fruit that is exceptionally sweet. Medium sized fruit.
Sources: Available from Daleys.

Pink Jerusalem - see Jerusalem, Pink

 Poileus Blanche

Listed in Goodman's Wholesale Fruit Catalogue of 1909 to 1914. No description. Lost.

Preston

Provenance: unknown, but probably related to 'Preston Prolific'.
Skin colour: Greenish-brown
Pulp colour: white
Description: Somewhat hairy, large fruit of high quality.
Breba Crop: unknown
Other information: Seems to have trouble maturing. Ripens December to April (southern hemisphere), vigorous grower.
Tree Sources (as of publication date): The Food Forest.

---

3   *Western Australian Nut And Tree Crop Association (a wonderful organisation, now unfortunately defunct).*

 Preston Prolific

Synonyms: Preston's Prolific

Provenance: Preston Prolific is believed to be a seedling of Black Genoa. It originated in Victoria, Australia, in the 1960s. In 1974 it was listed by Ikin in the Victoria and New South Wales state fruit collections.

Skin colour: green when immature, changing through straw-yellow to purplish brown when fully ripe.

Pulp colour: The flesh (the layer between the skin and the pulp) is creamy white. The pulp is amber coloured, sometimes tinted red.

Description: The somewhat hairy, large, high quality fruits are oblate, borne on a short stalk. Trees sold by Flemings under this name have fruit that is round and flattened with no neck, or slightly turbinate. The flesh is very thick and juicy, with a distinctive sweet flavour. Fruit splitting is not a problem. The fruit ripens mid to late-season and is usually harvested from February to March (southern hemisphere). When ripe the skin often tears around the stem.

Breba Crop: unknown.

Other information: A fig which has become popular in modern times, with a very good reputation as a jam maker The tree is vigorous with large leaves; fast-growing and self-fertile.

Tree Sources (as of publication date): Daleys, Bunnings, Greenpatch Organic Seeds, Hargraves' Nursery, Yalca.

 Provence, Black

Synonyms: Marseillaise Black, Black Marseilles, Marseillaise Negra, Reculver; Noir de Provence, Black Province.

Conflicts: Blanche Royale?

Provenance: France

Skin colour: Brown-black

Pulp colour: Red

Description: In 'The Fruit Manual', Robert Hogg writes: 'Small or below medium size, oblong. Skin, dark brown. Flesh, red, tender, very juicy, and richly flavoured. Tree bears abundantly, and is well adapted for forcing.' Crichton describes this as 'a French variety with roundish oblong fruit rather below medium size. Skin brownish black. Flesh red, tender very sweet and luscious. Ripens rather early The tree is hardy and bears prolifically.'

Breba Crop: unknown.

Other information: Grown by the R.H.S.V. in the 1890's at Burnley. Offered in Goodman's Fruit Catalogue of 1911; Sold by Law Sumner & Co in 1915. Probably Blanche Royale. Known only from the wax replica at the Science Works Museum in Victoria. Not referred to in any other literature. Lost

Provence, Blue

Synonyms: Blue Province.

Provenance: Probably from France, judging by the name. Offered in Goodman's Fruit Catalogue of 1911 to 1915.

Skin colour: Blue

Flesh Colour: Blue-purple

Description: Brunning's catalogue of 1916 describes it as having large fruit with a true blue skin colour, ripening late. According to Ikin in the N.S.W., fruit collection in 1974. Rance says that it is a mid-season variety with 'squat pyriform shaped fruit with a blue/violet skin showing prominent ribs, an open eye and blue tinged/purplish meat with red seeds. Very soft and sweet.'

Breba Crop: unknown.

Other information: Rare fig variety, once grown more widely in Australia, offered for sale in in this country occasionally. The tree is large and vigorous with exceptional large ornamental leaves. Ripens mid- to late-season. The tree has very large, ornamental leaves.

Tree Sources (as of publication date) Yalca, Daleys.

Provence, Brown

Mentioned in the Horsham Times in Victoria, 1894. Now lost.

Provence, White

Synonyms: Sugar Fig.

Valuable tree, producing a lot of fruit over a long period, beginning in January.[4] Whereabouts unknown.

Purple

This fig was obtained by a Western Australian grower, who passed on some cuttings to private growers in Victoria. Nothing else is known about it, as yet.

Purple Vigilante

'The Purple Vigilantes' is a 1938 American Western film. This fig was obtained by a Western Australian fig collector, who passed on some cuttings to private growers in Victoria. Nothing else is known, as yet.

Recourse Noir

Once grown at the Royal Horticultural Gardens, Richmond Park, Burnley, Victoria, in 1896. Whereabouts now unknown.

Rocardi

Once grown at the Royal Horticultural Gardens, Richmond Park, Burnley, Victoria, in 1896. Whereabouts now unknown.

---

4   Shum, c. 1950

 Royale Blanche

Once grown at the Royal Horticultural Gardens, Richmond Park, Burnley, Victoria, in 1896. Whereabouts now unknown.

Royale Vineyard

Once grown at the Royal Horticultural Gardens, Richmond Park, Burnley, Victoria, in 1896. Whereabouts now unknown.

Sandpaper fig - 'Bird's Eye'

Provenance: This is the only Australian native fig listed in this publication. 'Bird's Eye' is a selection of Ficus coronata, the Sandpaper Fig.

Skin colour: Purplish-black

Pulp colour: Red

Description: Large, oval fruits.

Breba Crop: Not applicable

Other information: Bird's Eye is an outstanding selection with large, flavoursome fruit. Heavy cropping and no splitting in wet weather. This small-growing tree with attractive sandpapery leaves occurs along watercourses along the east coast of Australia. Ideal fig selection for wet coastal areas. Excellent for creek bank stablilisation. Grows densely in full sun, less so in shade.

Tree Sources (as of publication date): Daleys.

Ficus coronata 'Bird's Eye'. Image: Daleys.

 San Pedro

Provenance: Grown at the Royal Horticultural Gardens, Richmond Park, Burnley, Victoria, in 1896. Somewhat confusingly, this cultivar belongs to a category of figs which bears the same name [see 'Fig Types']. 'Intermediate (or San Pedro) figs set an unpollinated breba crop, but need pollination for the later main crop.' However the Permaculture Melbourne 'lost figs' list states that the San Pedro cultivar was of the 'Smyrna type. It also states that San Pedro was 'not the same as Black Genoa'. The reason for this qualification is that Black Genoa was sometimes wrongly called 'San Pedro'.

Skin colour: Yellow-green

Pulp colour: Amber, tinged strawberry.

Description: Fruit medium to large, turbinate, Facciola states, 'main crop figs have less flavour'.

Breba Crop: good.

Other information: Glowinski describes this cultivar as 'best in hot dry climates' (Glowinski 1991). Whereabouts unknown.

 Schomburgk

This fig was obtained by a Western Australian grower, who passed on some cuttings to private growers in Victoria. Nothing else is known, as yet.

Moritz Richard Schomburgk (1811–1891) was the director of the Adelaide Botanic Gardens 1865-1891. It is probable that this cultivar was named after him.

 Sicilian, Black

Synonyms: Sicilian, Sal's, Sal's Fig, Corleone, Fico Di Capo, Fico Nera, Verna Grosso, Agrigenta.

Skin colour: Black

Pulp colour: Red

Description: Medium-large fruit, very juicy and sweet.

Breba crop: Yes

Currently growing in private collections in Australia.

 Silvan Beauty

Provenance: Discovered growing in the Silvan area of the Dandenong Ranges, near Melbourne, Victoria.

Skin colour: Purple

Pulp colour: Orange

Description: good flavour and heavy bearer, useful jam fig, harvests late season, tree can grow quite large

Tree sources: Yalca and Bulleen Art And Garden.

 Singleton Perpetual

Once grown at the Royal Horticultural Gardens, Richmond Park, Burnley, Victoria, in 1896. Whereabouts now unknown.

 Skoss

Skoss is listed by Hart as growing at Hillside Farm, W.A., in 2001. In fact, Hart lists Skoss cultivars numbered 1 to 5 and adds, 'Stock originally derived from importations from U.S.A. via N.S.W.' One cultivar named 'Skoss' is currently grown by private Australian collectors.

Small Brown Honey

Currently grown by private Australian collectors. No other information is available.

Smyrna

Synonyms: Calimyrna, Sanlop, Sarilop, Banana, Long Of August.

Provenance: The Smyrna figs [see page 3] were originally a traditional Greek type from the Meander valley near Ephesus/Smyrna in what is now Turkey. The 'Smyrna-types' include the popular Turkish cultivar known as 'Sarilop' in Turkey and 'Calimyrna' in the United States.

Like 'San Pedro', the cultivar 'Smyrna' shares a name with an entire category of figs. Facciola says of Smyrna that it is a 'class' of fig not a specific cultivar.' Nonetheless, one particular fig of this type became known as 'Smyrna'. In Australia it was offered for sale in fruit catalogues by Railton in 1880. In 1896 it was recorded as growing at Burnley by the Royal Horticultural Society of Victoria. Goodman's offered it for sale in 1911, Nobelius in 1931, and Levian in the early 20th century. Smyrna was also listed by Ikin as being in the N.S.W., South Australia and Victorian state fruit collections in 1974.

To add to Smyrna's Australian fame, some time between 1873 and 1960 it was faithfully replicated in three dimensions by being modelled in wax and hand-painted. One of more than 1800 realistic wax fruit and vegetable models, it is currently exhibited the Scienceworks Museum, 2 Booker St Spotswood, Victoria, Australia.

Skin colour: Yellow

Pulp colour: amber to light strawberry.

Description: A fruit of medium size, very sweet. Its skin turns from pale green to golden yellow when ripe and it has strawberry to red pulp. Can be glazed, eaten fresh, dried or made into jam.

Breba crop: usually either light or none.

Other information: One of the fig trees most resistant to frost. In the 1920s, caducous (Smyrna) fig varieties including the Smyrna cultivar and the numbered Calimyrna cultivars were commonly grown for dried fruit production in the MIA (the Murrumbidgee Irrigation Area in N.S.W.) and the Sunraysia area of Victoria. Production of dried Smyrna figs is not common now. Culture of Smyrna figs declined in the 1950s, when imported figs began to dominate the market.

Spanish Dessert

Provenance: Another variety that was in the South Australian collection at Loxton and was bulldozed in the 1990's. Scion was rescued by S.A. Rare Fruits Association members and propagated.

Skin colour: spectacular dark purple skin.

Pulp colour: dark red.

Description: An attractive, late maturing cultivar that fruits over a long season, from March to May (southern hemisphere). Delicious tasting.

Other information: Spanish Dessert is a cultivar of Smyrna, so it requires pollination by a caprifig if it is to produce fruit. 'It has an initially distressing habit of dropping large numbers of figlets on the ground, to the point that you think the tree will lose its whole crop, but as the tree settles down it bears good crops. It has rather luxurious dark green leaves making it a lovely landscape feature.'[5]

Sources: Grown privately by members of the Rare Fruit Society of South Australia and available from The Food Forest.

Striped Tiger - see Panachée

---

5   Quoted from *The Food Forest*.

 St Dominique

Once grown at the Royal Horticultural Gardens, Richmond Park, Burnley, Victoria, in 1896. Whereabouts now unknown.

St Dominique Violet

Provenance: Goodman's 1914 catalogue listed this as a 'large, dark violet fig.' It was also listed in an undated catalogue issued by Levian[6] & Son, 183-185 Elizabeth St. Melbourne, Victoria. It is probable that 'Violet' was a misspelling of 'Violette'.

St Dominique Violette

Synonyms: Saint Dominique Violette, St Dominique de Violette.

Provenance: A French cultivar listed in the report by George Neilson for the RVHS gardens at Burnley in 1875. Still being grown there in 1896. Listed in Goodman's Fruit Catalogues of 1905 - 1911, by Law Sumner in 1915 and in old mail-order catalogues up until the 1930s. Skin colour: dark violet/purple

Pulp colour: pink

Breba crop:

Description: Large fruit, great flavour.

Other information: There is a wax replica fig called "Saint Dominique Violet" at the Science Works Museum in Victoria. (Australia)

---

6   Levian may well have been the same H. F. Levian who, according to 'The Mildura Cultivator' of Saturday 28 September 1895, attended a Saturday evening meeting of 'representatives of the local fruit picking companies and agents'. The meeting was held at the offices of the Mildura Fruitgrowers' Association, 'the object being to consider the question of improving the marketing arrangements for the coming season's crop.'

Sources: In 2012 the Diggers Club Nursery, Dromana, Victoria, began offering this cultivar for sale accompanied by the words, 'Sourced from Phil Shepherd, whose family have been growing fruit trees in Victoria for three generations, this fig is one for the collector and connoisseur of fine fruits.'

St John

Synonyms: Saint John, Gillette.
Conflicts: Croisic, Cordelia, St Johns, Sant Jean, de Sant Jean,
Provenance: Once grown at the Royal Horticultural Gardens, Richmond Park, Burnley, Victoria, in 1896.
Skin colour: Pale green according to Figs 4 Fun, pale yellow according to the California Rare Fruit Growers, yellowish green according to Eisen.
Flesh Colour: white
Breba Crop: Yes, very sweet and juicy.
Description: An early ripener with excellent flavour.
'First crop: large, 2 1/2 inches (6.3 cm) long by 2 inches (5 cm) wide: pyriform; stalk medium, longer than the neck, which is not well set: skin smooth, waxy: ribs few, irregular; skin yellowish green, with numerous light specks of unequal size. Eye small, closed, with warty iris of the same colour as the fig: scales about six, large, pale dingy white: pulp and flesh white with small seed. Leaves medium, 5-lobed: end lobe the largest: lobes rounded deeply cut: stalks long.' Source: Eisen.
Other information: readily grown in pots. California rare Fruit Growers report: 'St John is the only edible caprifig. Fruits very early, only brebas are useful. Fruits are pale yellow, small, pulp is nearly white, without a lot of character. Tree is low, dense, spreading.'
Whereabouts in Australia now unknown.

 Stony Yellow

Synonyms: Stoney Yellow.

Currently grown by private Australian collectors. No other information is available.

 Sugar

Synonym: Celeste.

Skin colour: green

The Food Forest reports: 'Sugar Fig: is it another name for White Adriatic, the White Genoa or a separate variety? There is much confusion and misnaming of figs. Our Sugar Fig is great for jam and drying and is a medium-sized, sweet, green-skinned variety obtained from a local nursery!

See also Provence, White

Rare and Heritage Fig Cultivars

in Australia
T to Z

TENA

Synonyms: Tina, Teem, Col Di Signora Blanca.

Conflicts: Some information sources confuse 'Tena' with 'Col Di Signora Bianca' as grown by the Royal Horticultural Society of Victoria in the 1890's at Burnley; however 'Tena' was bred in the 20th century.

Provenance: One of Dr. Ira Condit's varieties which was produced by the fig breeding program at Riverside, California and were selected on the basis of being crack- and split-resistant. [See appendix: 'Hybridization of Caprifigs'.] Condit used Sari Lop (Calimyrna) as the mother. Named and released by Bill Storey in 1975. 'Tena' was listed by Hart as growing at Hillside Farm, W.A., in 2001.

Skin colour: Yellow or green-yellow

Flesh Colour: Pinkish/light strawberry

Description: Medium to large, with a roundish, oblate form and a small or non-existent neck. Similar to Mission but more rounded in shape. An early to mid-season fig, very sweet, fine flavour and of high quality. Delicious tender amber flesh. Some say the flavour resembles that of Mission. The flavour has been compared to that of a 'Fig Newton' biscuit. In hot, arid climates, figs may actually dry on the tree. Good for fresh use and for drying.

Breba Crop: good

Other information: Cold resistant to -14 °C. Good for warm climates. Widely adapted, but likes hot, dry weather. Vigorous and somewhat hardy. Tree somewhat spur-type. Very productive tree. Leaf: base truncate to decurrent; 3-5 lobes, lineate; central lobe elongated; margins crenate. Rance describes Tena: 'The tree is a strong grower with ascending branches and spur type growth; unusually long narrow deeply divided leaves.' Bears heavily. Tree strong, dense.

Sources (as of publication date): Private fig collections in Australia.

Tiger - see Panachée

 Todaro

A fig cultivar by this name was offered for sale by Yalca Fruit Trees in 2012-2013. Nothing else is known about it.

 Toulousienne

Listed as growing at Burnley, Victoria, in 1896. Whereabouts unknown

 Trojan

Listed as growing at Burnley, Victoria, in 1896. Whereabouts unknown

Turkey, Black

South Australian Register 1890: 'Mr. R. Linton, Murray Downs, New South Wales, said he had been very successful in drying figs, and that these were as good as those imported. The Black Turkey was the best, but it was rather shy in bearing.'

It is possible that the journalist confused Black Turkey with Brown Turkey, because this cultivar is not mentioned in any other literature.

Nonetheless, Tony Stevens listed a 'Black Turkey' as being among his collection and it is now being grown privately.

 Turkey, Brown

Synonyms: Ashridge Forcing; Aubicon; Aubique Noire; Black Spanish; Blue Burgundy; Blue; Brown Italian; Brown Naples; Brown; Brunswick; California Brown Turkey; California Large Black; Common Blue; Early Howick; Eastern Brown Turkey; English Brown Turkey; Everbearing; Fleur de Red; Fleur de Rouge; Fleur Rouge; Harrison; Ramsey; Italian; La Perpetuelle; Large Black; Large Blue; Lee's Perpetual; Long Naples; Murrey; Negro Largo; Nisse; Purple; San Pedro Black; San Pedro; San Piero; Texas Everbearing; Violetta; Walton.

Provenance: Provence, France.

Skin colour: Brownish-purple

Pulp colour: Reddish-pink

Description: Fruit is medium to large and pear shaped, with prominent deeply coloured ribs and a large, open eye. The skin is purplish brown and lighter at the stem end. The flesh is pinkish brown with an excellent flavour. Best eaten fresh, though excellent for jam. The nearly seedless reddish pink pulp is exceptionally tasty with a mild sweet flavour. The fruit of the early crop is quite large in size. The fruit is susceptible to souring during wet weather in coastal areas, but is reasonably resistant to splitting. This variety is highly recommended due to its long ripening season compared to the other varieties. The good quality fruit is recommended for fresh eating in contrast to drying or preserving.

Breba Crop: Does not usually produce a breba crop.

Other information: Earlyish variety of fig, but bearing over a long period; February, March and April. Brown Turkey is a small, hardy tree with sparse foliage. It crops well in most situations. If the tree is planted in the ground and injured by spring frosts, it will still produce fair to good fruit on sucker wood the next season. In Australia this variety does better in the dry inland than in coastal areas, but a very hardy fig which copes well with difficult conditions. Prune for a heavier main crop.

Sources (as of publication date): Just about any nursery or garden centre.

Uley Black

From Tony Stevens' fig collection. Now in the hands of private growers. No other information available.

Uley White

From Tony Stevens' fig collection. Now in the hands of private growers. No other information available.

Vardigo

Donated to a Western Australian fig collector by a Mr Collins. Now in the hands of private growers. No other information available.

Verdognola

Listed as growing at Burnley, Victoria, in 1896. Whereabouts unknown.

 Verdal

Listed as growing at Burnley, Victoria, in 1896. Whereabouts unknown.

 Verdal De Valencesses

Listed as growing at Burnley, Victoria, in 1896. Whereabouts unknown.

 Vermissieque

Listed as growing at Burnley, Victoria, in 1896. Whereabouts unknown.

Violette de Bordeaux. - see Negronne

 Violette Grosse

Listed as growing at Burnley, Victoria, in 1896. A hand-painted wax replica of this cultivar exists at Melbourne's Science Museum in Spotswood, Victoria. Probably purple in colour. Whereabouts unknown.

 White Nicolina

Offered for sale by Yalca Fruit Trees in 2014.

Product Description: 'A new fig for us this year, but actually a rare breed now, one for the collectors, originally came to us from a grower in N.S.W., delicious figs, hardy trees.'

White Marseilles: see White Genoa.

 White Provenence

Listed as growing at Burnley, Victoria, in 1896. Whereabouts unknown. Probably a misspelling of 'White Provence'. See: Provence, White.

 White Pacific

Listed as growing at Burnley, Victoria, in 1896. Whereabouts unknown

White Adriatic: see Adriatic, White

White Genoa: see Genoa, White

White Ischia: see Ischia, White

White Provence: see Provence, White

 Williams Prolific

Listed as growing at Burnley, Victoria, in 1896. Whereabouts unknown

Williams

'Williams' was listed by Hart as growing at Hillside Farm, W.A., in 2001. This cultivar was later collected by a private grower in Western Australia and passed on to collectors in Victoria.

 Winter

This cultivar was collected from an unknown source by a private grower in Western Australia and passed on to fig collectors in Victoria.

References to a 'Winter' fig in the literature suggest it may be synonymous with Natalino, Christmas Fig, Della Cava, Pasquale, Kargigna or Tre Volte Kargigna.

Eisen states, 'Natalino is a fig which ripens very late all through the winter, withstanding the frost, at Naples, and ripening after the leaves of the fig tree have fallen. Probably identical with Kargigna.

The USDA report (1887) records: 'Kargigna — Medium or below medium, turbinate; skin thin, white; pulp amber. A rather early Dalmatian fig. of medium quality, good only for table, and hardly worthy of cultivation. Introduced into California by G. N. Milco. Possibly identical with Natalino.'

Ficus carica 'Winter', fruit unripe, cupped leaves. Australia, March 2014.

Notably, the leaves of the 'Winter' fig in Australian collections are shaped like a cupped hand. The young stems are dark reddish in colour and the fruit turns from green to purple well before it is ripe.

Yum Yum

Provenance: From a family-run nursery business in the Yarra Valley, Victoria, near North Wandin. The family has been growing figs in that location for 130 years. They do not remember the fig's origin and invented the name 'Yum Yum' when selling it to retail nurseries. This cultivar is said to thrive in the relatively cool climate of the Yarra Valley.

Good flavour. Ripens late March in the southern hemisphere. Skin is golden brown when ripe.

Sources (as of publication date): Bunnings and many nurseries around Victoria.

Zidi

Synonyms: Zida, Zita, Ziata

Conflicts: Smyrna

Provenance: Dr Ira Condit arranged the importation of this cultivar to the U.S.A. from Tunisia in the 1950s. In Tunisia it is extremely popular and widely grown. Rescued from oblivion in Australia by Neil Barraclough of Gippsland, and distributed to private growers.

Skin colour: Dark purplish black

Flesh Colour: Not known.

Description: This is a Smyrna-type fig. Shape oblong, size large. Famous in Tunisia for its high commercial value and outstanding taste when eaten fresh. Very productive with a high yield of heavy, sweet fruit.

Breba Crop: Not known.

Other information: In Tunisia, Zidi figs are mainly consumed fresh. A small portion of the crop is sun dried, and very small quantities are used for jam and alcoholic beverage production. Date of maturity in Tunisia: August. A single mature tree can produce up to 80 kilograms of fruit per season when grown in fertile coastal areas, where Zidi thrives. In such conditions it can produce individual fruits weighing up to 82 grams.

TONY STEVEN'S PROVISIONALLY NAMED, AS YET UNIDENTIFIED FIG CULTIVARS

Ackland Road
Adam's Pride ?
Barossa Cutleaf
Black Bush
Dunn
Evangelista
Elizabeth Street
Fifth Street
Gianini
Giant Triple Trunk
Holiday Delivery
Lancuba 1
Lancuba 2
Longo Next Door
Longo Early
M. Bynes
Milton Gazump
Mt Benson
Plum
Puglisi White
SE Carisbrook
Sevante
South West
Whitford ?
Williams' Other
Wirrabara
Yanorm

APPENDIX

THE SYNCONIA OF CAPRI FIGS

PROFICHI

Profichi synconia form on buds just above the scars of fallen leaves on the previous season's wood (like the breba crop). They develop from October through to December. At this time new shoots and leaves are forming on the tree. The synconia develop rapidly, and within three weeks the female flowers are ready for fertilisation. The male flowers do not produce pollen until early December. This pollen fertilises the edible fig varieties.

MAMMONI

Mammoni form on the new growth each year (like the main edible crop). Mammoni start to develop in early December when the profichi crop is almost over, and continue to grow through until late March – early April. Mammoni caprifigs do not shed pollen.

MAMME

Mamme start to develop in May, when the mammoni crop is almost over and the tree has started to become dormant. They form near the tips of the branch. They stay on the tree during winter, and develop fully in September when the female flowers of the profichi crop are receptive. The male flowers do not shed pollen. The main varieties used to pollinate Smyrna and San Pedro figs in California are Roeding, Samson and Stanford. It is important that the correct variety of caprifig is chosen to ensure that pollen from the profichi crop is available at the right time.

Fig Growing in N.S.W. - N.S.W. Department of Primary Industries, September 2002.

CAPRIFICATION

The process of caprification is complex. It involves the presence of both the fig wasp and the correct stage of fig on the caprifig tree.

Commercial Smyrna-type figs are pollinated in early summer with pollen from the profichi caprifig. If the female flowers are receptive, the wasp will also pollinate the female flowers of the mammoni caprifig at this time. The flowers will then form seeds, completing the reproductive cycle of both the caprifig and commercial trees.

The female wasp lays eggs in all the female flowers, pollinating at the same time. The larvae hatch and develop in flowers with short styles. The long-styled flowers develop seeds. Generally one caprifig tree is needed for every 15 to 20 Smyrna trees. Planting the caprifig trees within the block is not recommended, as pollination is not even: the trees closest to the caprifigs can be over-fertilised and split, and more distant trees may not be pollinated.

Caprifig trees should be planted in a separate block. The profichi caprifigs (with wasps) are picked and placed in wire baskets around the orchard when the first wasps start to emerge. Each basket needs to contain six or seven figs. The profichi need to be replaced every three days for about three weeks, as not all the synconia of the Smyrna figs are receptive at the same time. It is useful to have more than one variety of caprifig so that the pollination period is extended.

Fig Growing in N.S.W. - N.S.W. Department of Primary Industries, September 2002.

HYBRIDIZATION OF CAPRIFIGS

'The University of California has maintained a fig cultivar improvement program since 1922. The 'Conadria' and "DiRedo" cultivars were released to the industry from this program in the mid 1950s and the 'Tena' cultivar was selected and released in the mid 1970s.

'The key to the development of hybrid fig seedlings that are persistent or of the 'common' type came in 1942 when Dr. Ira Condit discovered a unique type of caprifig growing at Cordelia, California. This caprifig, thought to be a European cultivar named 'Croisic' (syn: Cordelia, St. John, Gillette), was parthenocarpic, edible and could pass on the persistent characteristic to a portion of a seedling population developed from it.

'In time, through the efforts of Dr. William Storey, the Cordelia caprifig was improved through hybridization. By the late 1970s, three superior persistent caprifigs had been identified for use as pollen parents, each bearing heavy loads of fruit with green skin, white meat and amber pulp. One of the caprifigs contained genes of the Calimyrna cultivar.

'By the late 1980s, with additional hybridization, four new persistent caprifigs had been identified by James Doyle, each containing a varying percentage of the Calimyrna genome.'

Fig Cultivar Development And Evaluation, J. F. Doyle and L. Ferguson, Department of Pomology, University of California, Davis CA 95616, U.S.A. Date: circa 2000.

Note: Dr. Ira Condit selected his cultivars on the basis of being crack- and split-resistant. Most have a small eye. All have very high sugar content and are very resistant to decay.

PETER GOOD

'Peter Good (date of birth unknown, died 12 June 1803) was the gardener assistant to botanist Robert Brown on the voyage of HMS Investigator under Matthew Flinders, during which the coast of Australia was charted, and various plants collected.

'Good had worked as a foreman at Kew Royal Gardens [UK], during which time he had assisted botanist Christopher Smith in transporting a shipment of English plants to Calcutta.

He was working as a kitchen gardener at Wemyss Castle, Scotland, when Joseph Banks offered him the appointment as gardener to Brown, at a salary of £105 a year.

'Good made an extensive seed collection during the voyage, and also collected plant specimens for both his own and Brown's collections. He died during the voyage, and his plant collection was incorporated into Brown's.

'Brown immensely admired his work ethic, and named the plant genus Goodia in his honour. Banksia goodii (Good's Banksia) is also named after him.'

Wikipedia: 'Peter Good'. Retrieved March 2014.

THE PANACHÉE FIG - A SECTORIAL CHIMERA

A plant is said to be a chimera when cells of more than one genotype are found growing next to each other, in the tissues of that plant. Chimeras arise when a cell undergoes mutation. This mutation may be spontaneous or it may be induced by irradiation or treatment with chemical mutagens. In the case of the Panachée fig, the mutation was spontaneous; it happened naturally, without human intervention. This mutation is responsible for Panachée's striking gold and green stripes.

Plants often exhibit their chimerical nature by showing a variegation in colours; nonetheless, in theory a plant could be a chimera for virtually any trait. Other frequent chimeras involve loss of epidermal appendages ('thornless' blackberries, 'fuzzless' peaches), alteration in bract colour (such as in poinsettias), and various petal or flower color patterns in carnations and chrysanthemums.

There are three types of chimeras - periclinal, mericlinal, and sectorial. Panachée is sectorial.

'Sectorial chimeras result from mutations which affect sections of the apical meristem, the altered genotype extending through all the cell layers. This chimeral type is unstable and can give rise to shoots and leaves which are not chimeras. Both normal types and mutated types can be produced, depending upon the point on the apex from which the shoots differentiate.'

Source: 'Origin, Development, and Propagation of Chimeras.' R. Daniel Lineberger, Professor of Horticulture, Department of Horticultural Sciences, Texas A&M University. Date unknown.

W.A.N.A.T.C.A.

'The Western Australian Nut and Tree Crop Association was brought into existence in 1975 by a small group of people passionate about growing nut trees (the original name was the Western Australian Nutgrowing Society).

'A few years later, fruit and other tree crops were added to the brief. At that time, the variety of nut and fruit trees available to the public was very limited, as was information about the horticulture of growing and propagating exotic plants and the use and processing of their products.

'The Association flourished, with four meetings per year, plus field trips and other events. Quandong magazine was a quarterly newsletter that grew into a substantial publication: the last ten issues are presented here. The twenty-seven Yearbooks contained more detailed articles. Digitization is now complete.

'ACOTANC, the Australasian Conference on Trees and Nut Crops, was twice hosted by WANATCA in Perth, Western Australia. Papers from the ninth conference in 2001 are displayed on this website.

'In 2007, WANATCA was dissolved due to falling membership. There are now many more species and varieties of fruit and nut plants available and a great deal of information can be obtained on the internet. Unfortunately, it is now extremely difficult and expensive to import plant materials into Western Australia due to rigorous quarantine restrictions.

'Members of WANATCA felt that the information contained in these publications is of considerable value, so provisions have been made to ensure this material will continue to be available to the public.'

Source: www.quisqualis.com/WANATCA.html

BIBLIOGRAPHY

Barron, A. F. *New or Little-known Fruits*. Gardeners' Chronicle 27: 1192. November 23, 1867.
Grosse Verte Fig. Florist and Pomologist (ser.3) 1: 56. 1 figure.
Dola Madeleine Fig. Florist and Pomologist (ser.3) 1:179-81.1 figure.
A Selection of Choice Figs. Florist and Pomologist (ser.3) 1:211-13.

Baxter, Paul and Glen Tankard, *The Complete Guide to Growing Fruit in Australia* MacMillan , Melbourne, 1990.

Benson, Martin (Firm), *Benson's guide to fig culture in the open ground at the North: with instructions for open ground culture at the North of Japanese persimmons and pomegranates and catalogue of rare tropical fruits and plants : bananas, water lilies, etc., and also greenhouse and bedding plants, roses, fruit trees, etc*. Swanwick, Ill. :Martin Benson,1886.

Borg, J. *Cultivation and diseases of fruit trees in the Maltese Islands*. 622pp. Government Printing Office, Malta. (Fig, pp. 126-48.) 1922.

Brooks, R.M. and H.P. Elmo, *Register of New Fruit and Nut Varieties* UC Press, 1972

Brookman, Graham and Annmarie. *Fig Fact Sheet*. The Food Forest, Gawler, South Australia, 2009.

Brunnings, John & Sons *Descriptive Catalogue of Fruit Trees*. Somerville, Victoria, Australia. Undated but probably 1916.

Coles, John C. *Catalogue of Fruits* 1867-1874

Condit, I. J. *Fig Culture in California*. California Agriculture Extension Service Circular 77, 1933.
Fig Varieties: A Monograph. Hilgardia, February 1955

Crichton, D. A. *The Australasian Fruit Culturalist* Melbourne, 1893

D'Ounous, Léo 1863. *Les figuiers du sud-ouest*. Review Horticulturale. 34:59, 456-57.

Downing, A. J. *The Fruits and Fruit Trees Of America*. John Wiley, 2nd Edition, 1885.

Eisen, Gustav Ph. D. *The Fig: Its History, Culture, and Curing, with a Descriptive Catalogue of the Known Varieties of Figs*. Washington, 1901

Facciola, Steve. *Cornucopia, a Source Book of Edible Plants*. Kampong Press U.S.A.

George, Graeme and Barraclough, Neil. *Heritage Figs List: A list of varieties of figs compiled from the Goodmans Fruit catalogues of the early 1900s, the Brunnings catalogue of 1916 and records of the RHSV fig Collection at Burnley in 1896.*

Givan, Ray U. *Fig Varieties*. North American Fruit Explorers, Inc. 1997

Glowinski, Louis. *The Complete Book of Growing Fruit in Australia*. Lothian, 1992.

Goodman, C. J. *Wholesale Fruit Catalogues*. Bairnsdale, East Gippsland. 1900-1989.

Grey, W. G. *Fruit Catalogue*, Allwood Nursery Diamond Creek, Victoria, 1907. This catalogue lists nine varieties of which four were perhaps unique to this nursery.

Hankin, Bill. *Figs in Australia*. Prepared for the Heritage Seed Curators Australia, 2001.

Hart, Alex. *Problems Identifying Fig Varieties*. Paper presented at the Ninth Australasian Conference on Trees and Nut Crops, Perth, Western Australia, April 13-20, 2001

Hogg, Robert. *The Fruit Manual: a Guide to the Fruits and Fruit Trees of Great Britain*. 1884

Holmes, Roger (ed.) *Taylor's Guide to Fruits and Berries*. Haughton Miflin, 1996.

Ikin, R. Ph.D. *Varieties of Fruit Trees, Berry Fruit, Nuts and Vines in Australia*. Australian Government Publishing Service Canberra, 1974

Karp, David. *Farmers Markets: Panachée figs earn their stripes*. Los Angeles Times, August 09, 2013

Law Somner & Co; *General Catalogue of Garden Agricultural and Flower Seeds* 1915

Lord, E E. *Brunning's Australian Gardener 1957*. Angus & Robertson: Melbourne.

Neilson, George. *Three Reports on the Experimental Gardens to the Victorian Horticultural Society.at Burnley*. 1873, 1874, 1875.

Railton, James. *Seed & Plant List,* Melbourne, Victoria, undated but probably from the 1890s. In the 1870s Railton was John J. Coles' Melbourne agent, before starting his own business.

Rance, John. *The Fignificent Forgotten Fig.* S.A. Rare Fruit Society (date unknown).
The Loxton Fig Collection. South Australian Rare Fruit Society Newsletter 1997.

Shum, W. A. *Australian Gardening of Today.* Sun News Pictorial: Melbourne. Circa 1950.

Simon, C. *Fig Inventory.* University of California at Davis, Sept. 2000. (This inventory lists 120 fig varieties held at UCLA Davis and available to interested parties. Many are breeding lines that have been developed in the U.S.A. over the past 100 years. Some are heritage varieties no longer available elsewhere.)

Smith, Keith. *Growing Uncommon Fruits and Vegetables.* New Holland Publishers, Sydney, 1998

U.S. Department of Agriculture, Division of Pomology, Bulletin Vol. 1. *Report on the Condition of Tropical and Semi-Tropical Fruits in the United States III 1887. Catalogue and Description of Figs.* Published by Authority of the 8ecretary of Agriculture, Washington: Government Printing Office.

Whealy, Kent (ed.) *Fruit Berry and Nut Inventory 2nd Edition.* Seed Savers Publications, Decorah Iowa, U.S.A. 1993

Wyatt, C. W. *Descriptive List of Fruit Varieties.* Victoria 1874

FIGS IN AUSTRALIA

Name   Availability*   Colour

Name	Availability*	Colour
A Bois Jasper	N	Unknown
Adam	M	Purplish black
Adriatic, Black	N	Dark
Adriatic, White	Y	Greenish yellow
Agen	N	Greenish brown
Alma	M	Golden brown
Angélique	N	Unknown
Angélique Noir	N	Dark
Aubique Blanche	N	Pale
Aubique Noir	M	Purplish black
Archipal	Y	Greenish yellow
Ballona	N	Green
Bardajic	N	Green
Beck	M	Unknown
Belle Dame Blanche	N	Pale
Black Prince	M	Purplish black
Blanche Royale	N	Unknown
Bluet	N	Unknown
Bordeaux	N	Purplish black
Bourjassotte, Black	N	Purplish black
Bourjassotte, Blanche	N	Pale
Bourjassotte, Gris	N	Chocolate brown
Bourjassotte, Noir	N	Purplish black
Bourjassotte, White	N	Pale
Brown	Y	Brown
Brown Bell	M	Brown
Brown Sugar	M	Brown
Brunswick	M	Violet brown

* *Commercial availability as of March 2014: Yes, No, Maybe.*

Bull's No. 1	N	Unknown
Bultajik	N	Green
Calimyrna	M	Yellow
Cape White	M	Green
Capri	M	Unknown
Carmel Special	M	Yellow
Cassaba	N	Green
Castle Kennedy	N	Brown
Catalogna	Y	Dark purple
Celeste	M	Light bronze to violet
Chemeghour	N	Unknown
Citrus	M	Unknown
Clancy	M	Unknown
Clémentine	N	Unknown
Col Di Signora Blanca	N	Yellowish white
Col Di Signora Nero	N	Dark chocolate
Collins	M	Golden green
Collins Seedling	M	Unknown
Conadria	M	Yellow/green w. purple blush
Dalgety	M	Unknown
Datte	N	Pale green to brown
D'agen	N	Unknown
Deanna	M	Green to golden-yellow
De Lipari	N	Green tto golden-yellow
Desert King	N	Deep green, spotted white
De St Jeane	N	Unknown
De Quatre Saisons	N	Unknown
Don's Drying	M	Unknown
Don's Early	M	Unknown
D'or De Laura	N	Green to golden yellow
Dorée	N	Yellowish green to rose pink
Dr Hogg's Black	N	Dark mulberry
Dwarf Prolific	N	Unknown
Early Violet	N	Chocolate brown
Eileen Wilde	M	Unknown

Esperance Heritage	M	Unknown
Excel	Y	Yellow
Felice	M	Purplish-black
Ficarra	M	Unknown
Fiesta Di Desire	M	Unknown
Figue D'or	N	Unknown
Flanders	Y	Green
Florentine	M	Green
Genoa, Black	Y	Purplish black
Genoa, Large Black	N	Purplish black
Genoa, Large White	N	Pale yellow
Genoa, White	Y	Greenish-yellow
Good	M	Unknown
Gourande Rouge	N	Black
Gourandi	N	Unknown
Grossale	N	Unknown
Grosse Blanche De Marseilles	N	Unknown
Grosse Monstrueuse	N	Pale chestnut brown
Grosse Monstrueuse De Lipari	N	Pale chestnut brown
Grosse Rouge De Bordeaux	N	Unknown
Grosse Verte	Y	Green
Harold Jo	M	Unknown
Hasbargen Brown	M	Unknown
Hill's Large Brown	N	Unknown
Hollis Purple	M	Purple
Hollis White	M	Pale
Ischia	N	Unknown
Ischia, Black	M	Purplish-black
Ischia, Brown	M	Brown
Ischia, Green	M	Green
Ischia, Yellow	M	Yellow
Ischia, White	N	Green
Italian Honey	M	Greenish yellow
Jenny Smith Blue	Y	Purple to blue
Jerusalem	N	Green w. brown or violet blush

Jerusalem, Pink	M	Green
Kadota	M	Greenish yellow
King	M	Greenish yellow
Kungasava Strawberry	M	Unknown
Large Blue	N	Bluish purple
La Royale	N	Unknown
Lemon Lennie	M	Unknown
Lisbon	M	Unknown
Longue Blanche De Provence	N	Unknown
Lop Ingir	N	Yellow
Mackenwood	N	Unknown
Madeline	N	Pale yellow
Malta	N	Brown
Marseillaise	N	Unknown
Martin	M	Black
Martinique	N	Purplish black
Mary Lane	M	Green to yellow
Minorca Bianca	N	Green
Mission	M	Black
Monaco Blanche	N	Unknown
Monaco Bianco	N	Yellowish green
Mouissoune	N	Purplish black
Negronne	N	Purplish black
Negrone	N	Black
Negro Large	N	Black
Negro Largo	M	Dark
Negro De Espagne	N	Dark
Nepolitaine	N	Green
Nigra	N	Dark
Osborne Prolific	N	Dark bronze/reddish mahogany
Owen Special	M	Unknown
Oblique Blanche	N	Pale
Oeil De Perdrix	N	Unknown
Palane	N	Unknown
Panachée	M	Striped yellow and green

Paradise	M	Unknown
Peau Dure	N	Pale yellowish green
Persian Prolific	M	Light purple
Peter Good	M	Unknown
Picone	Y	Green
Poileus Blanche	N	Pale
Preston	Y	Greenish brown
Preston Prolific	Y	Purplish brown
Provence, Black	N	Brownish black
Provence, Blue	Y	Blue
Provence, Brown	N	Brown
Provence, White	N	Pale
Purple	M	Purple
Purple Vigilante	M	Purple
Recourse Noir	N	Unknown
Rocardi	N	Unknown
Royale Blanche	N	Unknown
Royale Vineyard	N	Unknown
Sandpaper Fig 'Bird's Eye'	Y	Purplish black
San Pedro	N	Yellow green
Schombergk	N	Unknown
Sicilian, Black	M	Black
Silvan Beauty	Y	Purple
Singleton Perpetual	N	Unknown
Skoss	M	Unknown
Small Brown Honey	M	Brown
Smyrna	M	Yellow
Spanish Dessert	Y	Dark purple
St Dominique	N	Unknown
St Dominique Violet	N	Violet
St Dominique Violette	Y	Violet
St John	N	Pale green
Stony Yellow	M	Yellow
Sugar	Y	Green
Tena	Y	Greenish yellow

Todaro	Y	Unknown
Toulousienne	N	Unknown
Trojan	N	Unknown
Turkey, Black	M	Purplish black
Turkey, Brown	Y	Brownish purple
Uley Black	M	Dark
Uley White	M	Pale
Vardigo	M	Unknown
Verdognola	N	Unknown
Verdal	N	Unknown
Verdal De Valencesses	N	Unknown
Vermissieque	N	Unknown
Violette Grosse	N	Probably purple
White Nicolina	M	Pale
White Provenance	N	Pale
White Pacific	N	Pale
Williams Prolific	N	Unknown
Williams	M	Unknown
Winter	M	Unknown
Yum Yum	Y	Golden brown
Zidi	Y	Purplish black

INDEX

A

A BOIS JASPER 26
ADAM 26, 27, 36, **119**
Adam's 26
Adriatic 28
Adriatic, xvi, 2, 27, 28, 36, 61, 108, 115
ADRIATIC, BLACK 27
Adriatic Hybrid 49
ADRIATIC, WHITE 28
Agen 30, 53
AGEN 30, 53
Agen D'Agen 30
Agrigenta 103
Albicougris 36
ALMA 30
ANGELIQUE 31, 60
Angélique Black 36
ANGELIQUE NOIR 31, 60
Angélique Noir 60
Angélique Noire 36
Arachipel 32
Archipal 32, 33, 92
ARCHIPAL 32, 33, 92
Archipel 32, 92
Ashridge Forcing 112
Aubicon 112
AUBIQUE BLANCHE 32
AUBIQUE NOIR 32
Aubique Noire 36, 89, 112
Aubique Violette 36
Aubiquon 36

B

BALLONA 34
Banana 104
Bardajic 40
BARDAJIC 34, 40, 44
Bardajik 34, 40
Barnissoto 37
Barnissotte 37
Bayswater 39
BECK 18, 35
Becks 35
Beer's Black 82
Belle Dame Blanche 35, 39
BELLE DAME BLANCHE 35, 39
Bellegrade 37
BETADA 35
Biberaeo 82
Black Adam 26, 36
BLACK ADRIATIC 27
Black Barnisaotte 37
Black Barnissotte 37
Black Bourjassotte 37, 38
BLACK BOURJASSOTTE 37
Black California 82
Black Geneva 62
BLACK GENOA 36, 62
BLACK ISCHIA 36, 70
Black Ishi 70
Black Marseilles 98
Black Martinique 80
Black Mexican 82
Black Mission 82
Black Naples 39
BLACK PRINCE 35
Black Provence 36, 70

BLACK PROVENCE 36, 98
Black Province 98
BLACK SICILIAN 36, 103
Black Spanish 89, 112
BLACK TURKEY 36, 111
BLACK, ULEY 113
Blanche 31, 32, 33, 35, 36, 37, 39, 42, 64, 65, 73, 78, 79, 86, 93, 97, 98, 99, 101
Blanche Royale 36, 98, 99
BLANCHE ROYALE 36, 98, 99
Blue 8, 46, 70, 74, 77, 99, 112
Blue Burgundy 112
Blue Celeste 46
Blue Ischia 70
BLUE PROVENCE 99
Blue Province 99
BLUET 36
BONDANCE PRECOCE 36
Bordeaux 31, 36, 66, 82, 87, 114
BORDEAUX 31, 36, 66, 82, 87, 114
Boughton 39
Bourgassotte Noire 37
Bourjassotte 37, 38, 94
BOURJASSOTTE, BLACK 37
BOURJASSOTTE BLANCHE 37
BOURJASSOTTE GRIS 38
BOURJASSOTTE NOIR 38
BOURJASSOTTE, WHITE 38
Bracotedesco 94
Brebal 82
Brogiotto Fiorentino 37
Brogiotto Nero 37
Broqiotto Nero 37
Brown xvi, 2, 32, 38, 39, 46, 63, 67, 71, 77, 79, 89, 98, 100, 104, 111, 112, 113, 124
BROWN xvi, 2, 32, 38, 39, 46, 63, 67, 71, 77, 79, 89, 98, 100, 104, 111, 112, 113, 124

BROWN BELL 39
Brown Hamburgh 39
BROWN ISCHIA 38, 71
Brown Italian 112
Brown Naples 112
BROWN PROVENCE 100
BROWN SUGAR 39, 46
Brown Turkey xvi, 2, 32, 38, 39, 46, 63, 77, 89, 111, 112, 113
BROWN TURKEY 38, 89, 112
Brunswick 35, 39, 45, 48, 112
BRUNSWICK 35, 39, 45, 48, 112
BULL'S NO. 1 40
BULTAJIK 40
Burnley Horticultural Gardens 9

C

California 2, 28, 30, 33, 37, 40, 49, 53, 54, 58, 59, 61, 66, 75, 76, 77, 79, 80, 81, 82, 85, 107, 110, 112, 116, 121, 123, 128, 130
California Black 82
California Brown Turkey 112
California Large Black 112
Californian Large Black 82
Calimyrna 2, 40, 41, 53, 78, 85, 104, 105, 110, 123
CALIMYRNA 40
CAPE WHITE 42
CAPRI 27, 43
Caprification 43
Caramel Special 43
CARMEL SPECIAL 43
CASSABA 44
Cassabah 44
CASTLE KENNEDY 44, 45
CATALOGNA 45
Celeste 39, 46, 47, 67, 68, 108
CELESTE 39, 46, 47, 67, 68, 108

Celeste Violette 46
Celestial 46
Charlie 54, 77
CHEMEGHOUR 47
Chico 28
Christmas Fig 116
CITRUS vi, 47
CLANCY 47, 48
Clementine 39
CLÉMENTINE 48
Col di Signora 48, 94
Col Di Signora Blanca 48, 110
COL DI SIGNORA BLANCA 48, 110
COL DI SIGNORA NERO 48
Cole, John J. 8
COLLINS 19, 49, 113
COLLINS SEEDLING 49
Common Blue 112
Conadria 32, 61
CONADRIA 32, 49, 50, 61, 64, 123
Conant 46
Contessina 49
Cordelia 49, 107, 123
Corleone 103
Coucourelle Blanche 31
Courgette 94
Croisic 49, 107, 123

D

D'AGEN 53
DALGETY 52
Dalmation Fig 28
DATTE 52
Dattero 76
Dauphine 26, 27
Deana 53
Deane 53
DEANNA 53
Deanne 53

De Bellegarde 37
De Gerusalem 74
De Jerusalem 74
De L'archipel 32
De Lipari 54, 65, 66
DE LIPARI 54, 65, 66
Della Cava 116
DE QUATRE SAISONS 55
de Sant Jean 107
Desert King 54, 77
DESERT KING 54, 77
De St. Jean 39
DE ST. JEANE 55
Di Gerusaleme 74
DON'S DRYING 55
DON'S EARLY 55
D'OR DE LAURA 55
Doree 56
Dorée 56, 60
DORÉE 56
Dottato 56, 59, 76
DOTTATO 56, 59, 76
Dottato Hybrid 59
Douro Nebra 82
Drap d'Or 39
DR. HOGG'S BLACK 57
DWARF PROLIFIC 57

E

Early Forcing 70
Early Lemon 31
EARLY VIOLET 58
Early Violette 58
Eastern Brown Turkey 112
EILEEN WILDE 58
English Brown Turkey 112
Erbeyli 40
ESPERANCE HERITAGE 59
Everbearing 112
EXCEL 59

F

Fall Gold 30
FELICE 60
FICARRA 60
Fico Averengo 52
Fico Datto 52
Fico De Fragola 28
Fico della Madonna 52
Fico Di Capo 103
Fico Genovese 52
Fico Larde 52
Fico Madama Rosso 52
Fico Nera 103
Fico Rossetto 52
Ficus barnissote 37
Ficus carica radiata 94
Ficus carica virescens 'Risso' 30
Ficus pachycarpa var. fasciata 94
FIESTA DI DESIRE 60
Figa Turca 94
Fig Characteristics 5
  Flavour 5
  Leaf shape 5
  Pulp colour 5
  Size and shape 5
  Skin colour 5
Fig Crops 6
Figo Bianco 73
Figs in Australia 8
Fig Types 3
  Caprifig 3
  Common Fig 4
  San Pedro 4
  Smyrna 3
Figue Aubiquoun 36
Figue de Bordeaux 36
Figue d'Or 31, 56
FIGUE D'OR 60
Figue Goutte 74
Figue Grise 32
Figue Poire 36
FLANDERS 61
Fleur de Red 112
Fleur de Rouge 112
Fleur Rouge 112
Florentine 62, 73, 76
FLORENTINE 62, 73, 76
Fracazzano 94
Fragola 28
Franciscan 82
Franciscana 82
Francisciana 82

G

Gasparrini 94
GENOA, BLACK 36, 62
GENOA, LARGE BLACK 63
GENOA, LARGE WHITE 64
GENOA, WHITE 64, 115
Gentile 76
Gerusalem 74
Gillette 107, 123
GOOD xvii, 7, 33, 46, 64, 65, 72, 76,
  87, 92, 97, 110, 117, 124
Goodman, John 8
Goodman's Catalogue 1910 8, 10,
  26, 35, 36, 38, 39, 63, 64, 65,
  67, 71, 78, 79, 93, 97, 99, 104,
  106, 129
Gourande Noir 65
GOURANDE ROUGE 65
GOURANDI 65
Gourand Noir 82
Gouraund Noir 82
Gourande diu Languedoc 82
Gourreau Noir 82
Goutte d'Or 56
GREEN ISCHIA 72
Green Packing Fig 78
Grise de la Saint Jean 55

Grizzly Bourjassotte 38
Grossagna 65
Grossagne 65
GROSSALE 65
Grossales 65
GROSSE BLANCHE DE MAR-
    SEILLES 65
Grosse du Draguignan 30
Grosse Monstreuse 66
Grosse Monstreuse De Lipari 66
GROSSE MONSTRUEUSE 54, 65,
    66
Grosse Monstrueuse De Lipari 54,
    65, 66
GROSSE MONSTRUEUSE DE
    LIPARI 54, 65, 66
GROSSE ROUGE DE BORDEAUX
    66
Grosse Rouge De Bourdeaux 36
Grosse Verdale 30
Grosse Verte 28, 67, 127
GROSSE VERTE 28, 67, 127
Grossofigo 37

H

Hankin, Bill viii, 8, 9, 11, 13, 15, 66
Hanover 39
Hardy Celeste 46
Hardy Prolific 32, 92
HAROLD JO 67
Harrison 112
Hart, Alex 12, 19, 40
HASBARGEN BROWN 67
Heritage Fruits Society 14
HILL'S LARGE BROWN 67
HOLLIS PURPLE 68
HOLLIS WHITE 68
Honey 32, 46, 68, 76
Honey Fig 62, 73, 78, 79

I

Improved Blue Celeste 46
ISCHIA xvi, 36, 38, 70, 71, 72, 73,
    115
Ischia Black 70
ISCHIA, BLACK 36, 70
ISCHIA, BROWN 38, 71
ISCHIA, GREEN 72
ISCHIA, WHITE 73, 115
ISCHIA, YELLOW 72
Italian 10, 28, 30, 32, 43, 48, 52, 54,
    60, 62, 65, 66, 68, 70, 72, 73,
    77, 78, 79, 94, 112
Italian Golden 73
Italian Honey 32, 62, 68, 73, 78, 79
ITALIAN HONEY 32, 62, 68, 73,
    78, 79
Italian Large Blue 77
Italian Strawberry 28
Italian White 30

J

Jaspée 94
Jaspee Limone 94
Jelly 81
JENNY SMITH BLUE 74
JERUSALEM xvi, 74, 75, 97
JERUSALEM, PINK 75, 97

K

Kadota 56, 59
KADOTA 2, 50, 56, 59, 76
Kadota Hybrid 59
Kargigna 116
King 8, 54, 77
KING 8, 54, 77
KUNGASAVA STRAWBERRY 77

L

La Perpetuelle 112
L'archipel 32
Large Black 63, 82, 112
LARGE BLACK GENOA 63
Large Blue 8, 77, 112
LARGE BLUE 8, 77, 112
LARGE WHITE GENOA 64
Large White Turkey 39
La Royale 73, 78
LA ROYALE 73, 78
Lattarula 32, 64, 73
Lattarula, 32, 73
Lee's Perpetual 112
Lemon 31, 32, 64, 73, 78
LEMON LENNIE 78
LISBON 78
Little Brown 46
Little Brown Sugar 46
Lob Ingir 78, 79
Lob Injir 40
Long Naples 112
Long of August 104
LONGUE BLANCHE DE
    PROVENCE 78
Lop 40, 78
LOP INGIR 78, 79
Lucrezia 48

M

MACKENWOOD 79
Madeleine 31, 79, 127
Madeleine, 31
MADELINE 79
Madonna 39
Magnolia 39
Malta 46, 94
MALTA 46, 79, 94, 127
Maravilla 94

Marbled Limone 94
MARSEILLAISE 80, 98
Marseillaise Black 98
Marseillaise Negra 98
Marseilles 64, 80
MARTIN 80, 127
MARTINIQUE 80, 81
Mary Jane 81
Mary Jane Jelly 81
MARY LANE 81
Melette 31
MINORCA BIANCA 82
MISSION 2, 6, 36, 60, 82, 83, 84, 85,
    87, 110
Monaco Bianco 86
MONACO BIANCO 86
MONACO BLANCHE 86
MOUISSOUNE 86
Murrey 112

N

Napolitaine 38, 89
Napolitano 89
Natalino 116
Neapolitan 89
Nebian 28, 67
Negra 82, 98
NEGRO DE ESPAGNE 89
Negro d'Espagne 62
NEGRO LARGE 88
Negro Largo 88, 89, 112
NEGRO LARGO 88, 89, 112
NEGRONE 88
Negronne 36, 82
NEGRONNE 36, 82, 86, 87, 88, 114
Neilson, George 9
NEPOLITAINE 89
Nero 37, 48, 70
Neveralla 33, 92
Nigra 62

NIGRA 62, 89
Nisse 112
Noir de Provence 98
Noire de Languedoc 62
Noire d'Espagne 82

O

OBLIQUE BLANCHE 93
OEIL DE PERDRIX 93
Osborn 33, 92
Osborne 33, 92
OSBORNE PROLIFIC 92
Osborne's Prolific 92
Osborn's Prolific 33
Other Australian fig collections 18
OWEN SPECIAL 93

P

PALANE 93
Panache 94
PANACHÉE 94
Panachie 94
PARADISE 96
Pasquale 116
PEAU DURE 96
Peldure 96
Père Hilarion 94
PERSIAN PROLIFIC 96
Pests and Diseases 7
PETER GOOD 97
Petite Aubique 36
Petite Figue Grisé 31
PICONE 45, 97
Piconi 97
PINK JERUSALEM 75, 97
Plume 94
POILEUS BLANCHE 97
Porter, Deborah viii, 18
Precoce Noire 37
PRESTON 2, 97, 98

PRESTON PROLIFIC 2, 97, 98
Preston's Prolific 97, 98
PRINCE, BLACK 35
Princessa 94
Propagation 6
PROVENCE, BLACK 36, 98
PROVENCE, BLUE 99
PROVENCE, BROWN 100
PROVENCE, WHITE 100, 108, 115
Purple 44, 68, 74, 83, 100, 103, 112
PURPLE 44, 68, 74, 83, 100, 103, 112
PURPLE VIGILANTE 100

Q

R

Ramsey 112
Rance, John viii, 10, 13, 14, 16, 78
Rare Fruit South Australia 10
Rayée 94
Rayonne 94
RECOURSE NOIR 100
Reculver 82, 98
Red xiv, 39, 49, 80, 98, 101, 103, 112
Rigato 94
Risso 30, 32, 94
ROCARDI 100
Ronde Noire 32, 70
Royale 36, 73, 78, 98, 99, 101
ROYALE BLANCHE 101
ROYALE VINEYARD 101
Royal Victorian Horticultural
    Society 8
Rust 32, 92

S

Saint Dominique Violette 106
Saint John 107
Sal's 103
Sal's Fig 103
SANDPAPER FIG 'BIRD'S EYE' 101
Sanlop 104
San Pedro 3, 4, 6, 26, 27, 45, 54, 62, 77, 102, 104, 112, 121
SAN PEDRO 3, 4, 6, 26, 27, 45, 54, 62, 77, 102, 104, 112, 121
San Pedro Black 112
San Piero 62, 66, 89, 112
Sant Jean 107
Sarilop 104
Sari Lop 40, 110
Sari Lopi 40
SCHOMBURGK 102
Seedless 81
Sicilian 36, 103
SICILIAN, BLACK 36, 103
SILVAN BEAUTY 103
SINGLETON PERPETUAL 103
Site and Soil Requirements 6
SKOSS 103
Small Brown 79, 104
SMALL BROWN HONEY 104
SMYRNA 3, 4, 8, 40, 41, 43, 44, 70, 102, 104, 105, 117, 121, 122
South Australian fig repository at Loxton 12
SPANISH DESSERT 105
ST DOMINIQUE 106
St Dominique de Violette 106
ST DOMINIQUE VIOLET 106
ST DOMINIQUE VIOLETTE 106
Stevens, Julie 16
Stevens, Tony 16, 18, 31, 47, 55, 58, 60, 61, 71, 72, 76, 77, 81, 85, 113
ST JOHN 107
St Johns 107
Stoneville Research Station 19
Stoney Yellow 108
STONY YELLOW 108
Strawberry 28, 46, 50, 53, 54, 58, 70, 72, 74, 77, 83
Strawberry Fig 28
Strawberry Jam Fig 28
Striped Signora 94
Striped Tiger 94, 105
Sugar 39, 46, 100, 108
SUGAR 39, 46, 100, 108
Sugar Fig 100, 108

T

Teem 110
TENA 49, 110, 123
Tennessee Mountain 46
Texas Everbearing 112
The Western Australian Nut and Tree Crop Association 12
Tiger 94, 105, 111
Tina 94, 110
Tina ta Spanja 94
TODARO 111
Tony Stevens' Fig Collection 16
TOULOUSIENNE 111
Tre Volte Kargigna 116
TROJAN 111
TURKEY, BLACK 36, 111
TURKEY, BROWN 38, 89, 112

U

ULEY BLACK 113
ULEY WHITE 113

V

VARDIGO 113
Variegato 94
Ventura 28
Verdal 30, 114
VERDAL 30, 114
Verdala 30
VERDAL DE VALENCESSES 114
Verdal Longue 30
VERDOGNOLA 113
Verdone 28, 49, 61, 67
Verdone Hybrid 49, 61
Verdonne 28
VERMISSIEQUE 114
Verna Grosso 103
Verte 28, 54, 67, 72, 127
Verte Petite 54
Violetta 112
Violette 36, 46, 58, 82, 87, 106, 114
Violette de Bordeaux 36, 82, 87, 114
Violette De Bordeaux 36
VIOLETTE GROSSE 114
Violette Longue 36

W

Walton 112
White xvi, 2, 8, 28, 29, 30, 32, 33, 39, 42, 48, 50, 61, 64, 67, 68, 70, 72, 73, 76, 77, 81, 100, 108, 113, 114, 115, 119
WHITE ADRIATIC 28
WHITE BOURJASSOTTE 38
White Endich 76
WHITE GENOA 64, 115
White Ischia 72, 115
WHITE ISCHIA 73, 115
White Kadota 76
White King 77
White Marseille 73
White Marseilles 32, 64, 73, 114
WHITE NICOLINA 114
WHITE PACIFIC 115
WHITE PROVENANCE 115
WHITE PROVENCE 100, 108, 115
WHITE, ULEY 113
WILLIAMS 115, 119
WILLIAMS PROLIFIC 115
WINTER xiv, 116, 117

X

Y

Yellow Excel 59
Yellow Ischi 72
YELLOW ISCHIA 72
YUM YUM 117

Z

Ziata 117
Zida 117
ZIDI 117, 118
Zigarella 94
Zita 117

SOME MAIL ORDER FIG RETAILERS IN AUSTRALIA

All Green Nursery, 130 Old Geelong Road, Hoppers Crossing, Vic. 3029.

Daleys Nursery, 36 Daleys Lane, Geneva via Kyogle, N.S.W. 2474.

Greenpatch Organic Seeds, 109 Old Bar Road, Glenthorne, N.S.W. 2430.

Hargraves' Nursery, 630 Old Northern Rd, Dural N.S.W. 2158.

The Diggers Club, PO Box 300, Dromana Victoria, 3936.

The Food Forest, PO Box 859, Gawler, South Australia, 5118.

Yalca Fruit Trees, P.O. Box 249, Nathalia Victoria, 3638.

SOME NON MAIL ORDER FIG RETAILERS

Telopea Mountain Permaculture & Nursery, 134 Invernay Rd., Monbulk, Vic. 3793. Contact www.petethepermie.com for opening times.

Bunnings Warehouse - Australia-wide.

Tass 1 Trees, 1072 Great Northern Highway Baskerville, Western Australia.

Newman's Nursery, 1361 North East Rd, Tea Tree Gully. S.A. 5097.

Some Heritage Fruit Groups in Australia

Werribee Park Heritage Orchard, situated near Melbourne, Victoria (Australia) is a beautiful antique orchard dating from the 1870s, on the grounds of the old mansion by the Werribee River. It was renowned for its peaches, grapes, apples, quinces, pears, a variety of plums and several other fruits, as well as walnuts and olives. Over the past few decades the orchard was forgotten and - through neglect - fell into ruin. Recently this historic treasure has been rediscovered. Volunteers are replanting and tending the orchard.

The Heritage Fruits Society is based in Melbourne, Australia. Their aim is to conserve heritage fruit varieties on private and public land. They enable and encourage society members to research this wide range of varieties and to inform the public on the benefits of heritage fruits for health, sustainability and biodiversity.

Petty's Orchard in Templestowe, Victoria, Australia, is one of Melbourne's oldest commercial orchards, and it holds the largest collection of heritage/heirloom apple varieties on mainland Australia, with more than two hundred varieties of old and rare apples. The maintenance of the apple tree collection is done by Heritage Fruits Society volunteers.

The Rare Fruit Society of South Australia is an amateur organisation of fruit tree growers who preserve heritage varieties, explore climate limitations and study propagation, pruning and grafting techniques.

www.ingramcontent.com/pod-product-compliance
Lightning Source LLC
Chambersburg PA
CBHW070948180426
43194CB00041B/1714